Crisis on Campus

Crisis on
Campus

A Bold Plan for Reforming
Our Colleges and Universities

Mark C. Taylor

Alfred A. Knopf   New York   2010

THIS IS A BORZOI BOOK
PUBLISHED BY ALFRED A. KNOPF

Library of Congress Cataloging-in-Publication Data
Taylor, Mark C., [date]
Crisis on campus : a bold plan for reforming our colleges and
universities / Mark C. Taylor.
p. cm.
Includes index.
ISBN 978-0-307-59329-0
1. Education, Higher—United States. 2. Educational
change—United States. I. Title.
LA227.4.T39 2010
378.72—dc22   2010001565

Manufactured in the United States of America

Published September 1, 2010

Second Printing, December 2010

For
Selma Linnea
and
Elsa Ingrid

All things are entwined, enmeshed, enamored.

—*Friedrich Nietzsche*

Contents

Crisis on Campus

1

Reprogramming the Future

American higher education has long been the envy of the world. Much of the most important research that has contributed to the advancement of knowledge and enrichment of human life historically has been conducted in our colleges and universities. In the years following World War II, increasing prosperity and enlightened government policies led to rapidly expanding undergraduate programs that created new opportunities for countless young people. But in the past four decades, this situation has gradually deteriorated. The quality of higher education is declining; colleges and universities are not adequately preparing students for life in a rapidly changing and increasingly competitive world. As emerging technologies continue to transform how we manage information and acquire knowledge, students will need to develop new skills and even learn different ways of thinking, reading and writing. The accelerating rate of globalization will make it necessary for people to learn more about other societies and cultures. These developments also pose new challenges and opportunities for the organization and delivery of higher education. Changes in how information is distributed and knowledge communicated will both create more competition in higher education and provide the occasion for new forms of cooperation at the local, national and even global level. While many regard these developments as a threat to the quality of American higher education, I believe they offer the possibility of greatly expanding and enriching educational opportunities for people not only in this country but throughout the world.

Meeting these challenges will not be easy. Entrenched interests on campuses across the country remain resistant to change and refuse to accept that fundamental transformations are not only necessary but unavoidable. The growing number of college and university faculty members focused on their research and publishing careers has led to a conflict between the preoccupations of professors and the needs of students. As the interests of those faculty members become more specialized and the subjects of their publications more esoteric, the curriculum becomes increasingly fragmented and the educational process loses its coherence as well as its relevance for the broader society. If this trend continues, a growing number of young people and their parents will begin to question the value of higher education.

These problems are compounded by mounting financial pressures that are making it considerably harder for students to afford higher education and for schools to remain on the cutting edge of research while at the same time providing high-quality teaching to a new and quite different student population. Parents, desperate to ensure their kids' futures, remortgage their houses to pay for college, only to have their young graduates return home and begin their working lives in run-of-the-mill service jobs. At the graduate level, universities are producing a product for which there is no market (candidates for teaching positions that do not exist) and developing skills for which there is diminishing demand (research in subfields within subfields and publication in journals read by no one other than a few like-minded colleagues). Many of our best and brightest spend eight to ten years chasing unfulfillable dreams. Graduate students who finally admit they have no future in higher education are often in their thirties, deeply in debt, and face a difficult challenge to reinvent themselves.

It is not only parents and students who are facing the prospect of financial crisis: the education bubble is about to burst. There are disturbing similarities between the dilemma colleges and universities have created for themselves and the conditions that led to the collapse of major financial institutions supposedly too secure to fail. The value of college and university assets (i.e., endowments) has plummeted. The schools are overleveraged, liabilities (debts) are increasing, liquidity is drying up, costs continue to climb, their product is increasingly unaffordable and of questionable value in the marketplace, and income is declining. This situation is not only unsustainable, but at the crisis point.

A vibrant educational system is essential for democracy to thrive and individuals to prosper in our globalized world. When information is the currency of the realm, education is more valuable than ever. The accumulation and transmission of information are necessary but not sufficient for the viability of higher education. Higher education, in my view, has a responsibility to serve the greater social good, and in today's world this can be accomplished most effectively by cultivating informed citizens who are aware of and open to different cultural perspectives and are willing to engage in reasonable debate about critical issues. In an age of vitriolic bloggers and contentious cable news shows, when even the pretense of objective journalism is thought unnecessary by many, colleges and universities have an obligation to provide an education that will broaden students' horizons, helping them to resist the temptation of oversimplification and bias and to sift through misinformation in a world that is ever more complex.

Having taught for many years at a distinguished liberal arts college (Williams) and more recently at a leading research university (Columbia), I have been worrying about the growing vulnerability of higher education for more than two decades. As financial markets spun out of control in late 2008 and early 2009 and most of the people who run higher education continued to be oblivious to the turmoil swirling around them, I published an op-ed essay in *The New York Times* entitled "End the University as We Know It." No article I have written provoked anything like the response to this piece. My analysis of the current state of higher education and proposals for change set off a firestorm of discussion and controversy. Within hours the essay was everywhere on the Internet—people were posting it on Facebook, and students reported to me that it was all over the popular blog Gawker. It was the most e-mailed article in the *Times* for four days and was on their top-ten list for a week. Bloggers were also quick to respond; indeed, the *Times* had to shut its blog when more than five hundred responses were posted on the first day. There were also responses in major blogs, including those sponsored by *The Huffington Post, The Chronicle of Higher Education, The Atlantic* and *Harper's*. I received hundreds of personal e-mails, and the op-ed was even translated and published abroad.

What struck me about the response was not only how overwhelming it was, but also the difference between the public and private reactions. Letters to the editor and comments on blogs—most of them written by academics—were not only critical but quite hostile. Academics defended their own interests, claiming that things are not nearly as bad as I portrayed them and insisting that my proposed changes would destroy higher education. The e-mails, by contrast, were from former, present and prospective students, parents and people who had dropped out of school or had been forced to leave academic life for some reason. These messages were 98 percent positive.

Many of these long and thoughtful e-mails gave me a valuable window into public perceptions that reinforced my sense of the widening chasm between the ivory tower and the world at large. While countless messages were moving, one in particular stands out. It was from a young woman named Rita Sophie Bragiuli, who was a senior at Northwestern University. She was interested in pursuing graduate work in the study of religion but was encountering problems that unfortunately are all too common.

I think your points for revision are obviously radical, but that many of them make a great deal of sense. I also think it is time for the academic community to realize that it must restructure itself. I certainly fear, though almost expect, that no one will actually read my work, and that it will go for naught, even if there is real world application to it. It seems to me as if universities as well as scholars are producing too much literature, yet saying too little, with very little synthesis of ideas.

The course of study which I have proposed is inherently interdisciplinary, and I can't begin to describe how difficult it has been for me to explain this. I plan to study religion through the lens of psychology, both experimental and theoretical. I'd like to understand the impact religious specifics (texts, philosophies, rituals, etc.) through history have on the mind of the religious individual today, and how that implicates this person's behavior (from belief to going to temple/church to conversion to acts of violence).

8

Though this study is extremely broad, and incorporates fields of religion, history, anthropology, ethnography, philosophy, and psychology, the tools to complete this study are out there, and can have real impact on how we understand the modern religious mind. In addition, I want to eventually make this study comparative. Both Harvard and [the University of] Chicago have told me that this plan is interesting, but that I will have to pave the interdisciplinary path if I intend to take from both major fields (religion and modern psychology) equally. Indeed, I still cannot find any advisor who studies something quite like this. Despite the fact that universities may not be ready to follow this route, from talking to many future graduate students and scholars I've realized that the younger generation is craving such connections as well as applicability. . . .

Finally, I completely agree with you about collaborative work and classes across universities. Just an anecdote from my own experience: though Northwestern and University of Chicago are both members of a collaborative group of midwestern universities, I could not find a way to take Sanskrit at the University of Chicago. I wasn't allowed to enroll in a graduate course exchange program because I did not already have a B.A., and I could not enroll as an undergraduate without applying to the college. As a result, I've been traveling to the University of Chicago twice a week to learn Sanskrit while receiving no credit and no official transcript. I am grateful to the professors there for realizing my predicament and letting me attend class anyway. However, it is this kind of barrier that would discourage the enthusiastic student who is simply interested in learning. . . .

The level of sophistication of this young woman and her projected plan of study are quite impressive. What she is proposing is the kind of work we should be encouraging rather than discouraging.

A few weeks later, a conversation I had with a student who was in the first class I taught at Williams and had returned for his thirty-fifth reunion reinforced the extent of the problems higher education is facing. After graduation, Harvey went to medical school, and he has become a leading heart surgeon in New Mexico. I have stayed in touch with him over the years and been impressed not only by his accomplishments as a physician but also by his commitment to deliver health care to individuals who cannot afford it. Harvey has developed an innovative program that uses the Internet and teleconferencing to provide medical services to Native Americans scattered on reservations throughout the state of New Mexico. He once told me that he would never have conceived such a program without the questions he encountered in Religion 101. When I pressed him to explain what he meant, he said, "You always stressed the importance of studying other religious and cultural traditions. We read *Black Elk Speaks,* and that book left a lasting impression on me. I still remember our discussion about the ethical questions raised about the treatment of Native Americans. When I moved to New Mexico, I decided to learn about the traditions of the tribes in the area. I spent some time on reservations and was appalled by the living conditions. So many people had serious health problems that I decided to find a way to help them." This comment stuck in my mind as a telling testimony to the value of liberal arts education.

A few days before his visit, I received an e-mail from Harvey.

I saw the op-ed you published in *The New York Times.* It really hit home; I couldn't agree more—significant changes are needed in college education but I would also add medical school. What you said about the fragmentation of knowledge really applies to medical education. Everybody is so specialized that people study only one organ, condition or disease and nobody ever considers the body as a whole, to say nothing about the social, economic, political and environmental conditions that are so important. I've been thinking about all of this because, believe it or not, my kids are beginning to look at colleges and I must say, it's pretty grim. So much of what they do in colleges today is completely irrelevant; it's not just that it's impractical but so much of it has little or nothing to do with the real world. People seem to have lost sight of the purpose of higher education. And on top of that there's the cost. By the time I pay for both my kids, I'll be out more than half a million dollars just for undergraduate college. If they want to go to law school or medical school add another three quarters of a million bucks. Even if they qualified, financial aid is drying up. I'm not sure how we are going to handle it.

A growing number of people share Harvey's concerns. Though the importance of higher education is generally recognized, there is widespread concern about its quality, relevance, affordability and accessibility. When I asked Harvey how the experience of his kids differed from his own, he responded,

So much has changed since I went to college. When I graduated from high school, I knew nothing about the world and had no idea what I wanted to do. College was an interlude before I was forced to get serious. Today, kids are exposed to so much so early. In some ways they know much more about the world than when I was their age. But in other ways they are even more confused than we were. They are bombarded with information but don't know how to assess or process it. And they are much more worried about their future than we were. I guess some of that is our fault—we are always putting pressure on our kids. We know that even if they get into a good college, their future will be far less secure than ours was.

While my life's experience has made me painfully familiar with many of the problems plaguing higher education, I do not pretend to know all the answers to the questions we face. I do know, however, that the status quo is not viable. I believe I have a new vision for higher education, one that builds on the strengths of existing institutions, while moving into a future rich with possibilities. My aim in writing this book is to begin a national conversation about transforming our institutions of higher learning. My hope is that students, parents, faculty members, college and university administrators, policymakers and people from all spheres of public and private life will begin a civil debate about how we can best prepare young people for the unprecedented challenges that lie ahead. We must discuss the elephant in the classroom openly and honestly: the system of higher education is in many ways broken and needs to be overhauled. Moments of crisis are also times of opportunity—if we have the courage to act creatively and imaginatively, we can improve the prospects not only for our citizens, but for untold others around the world, whose lives we could influence.

Though the changes needed are far-reaching, they can begin incrementally and widen over time. To proceed effectively, it is necessary to understand the broader setting in which this crisis has emerged. In the first chapters of this book, I provide the historical context and consider recent social, political, economic and technological developments that have led to our current impasse; in the later chapters, I present proposals for what I hope will be creative solutions. The organizational structure and operating principles that have formed the foundation of higher education for more than two hundred years no longer function effectively. New information, media and, most important, networking technologies are transforming global social, political and economic infrastructures in ways that are revolutionizing the production and transmission of information. As I have suggested, these technologies are not only producing vast quantities of information but also recasting the very structure of knowledge and the means of its dissemination. Lectures and seminars offered in today's colleges and universities are still similar in style and format to those delivered in classrooms in the 1700s, with professors—and, increasingly, adjuncts and graduate students—lecturing to hundreds of students who passively transcribe the spoken word like medieval scribes recording holy writ. Unfortunately, large classes are not going to disappear; to the contrary, classes will become considerably larger and the learning experience much more depersonalized in the future. Mounting financial pressures are already making smaller classes that allow for discussions between teachers and students as well as debate among students increasingly rare. It is, therefore, necessary to find other pedagogical strategies to promote the exchange of ideas that is vital to the educational process.

Though technology cannot solve all of our problems, it does have the potential to address some of our most urgent needs. For example, the use of synchronous and delayed online text-based discussions is already widespread. Newer technologies now make it possible to simulate real-time class discussions using multipoint video conferencing that connects people at different locations. Some of these products are commercial, but others can be used free of charge by institutions as well as individuals. While obviously not as desirable as the traditional face-to-face discussions, these technologies make it possible for faculty members to have contact with students outside the confines of the traditional classroom setting. It is going to become necessary for students to be less reliant on teachers and mentors and to assume more responsibility for their own education.

These developments should be undeniable to any interested observer, but many faculty members resist significant change and remain committed to obsolete areas of research and outdated pedagogical practices. This is, in my judgment, irresponsible. If colleges and universities will not transform themselves, it is incumbent upon the broader society to pressure them to provide the educational opportunities our children deserve and our country needs.

We are facing what Andy Grove, former CEO of Intel, aptly describes as a "strategic inflection point." Just as the industrial revolution of the late eighteenth and early nineteenth centuries displaced an agricultural economy with industrial capitalism, so at the beginning of the twenty-first century the network revolution is displacing industrial and consumer capitalism with global financial capitalism. It is important to recall that the emergence of industrialism was inseparable from the rise of the nation-state. The modern university was conceived and established to meet the codependent needs of the new industrial economy and emerging nation-states. Though the interrelation of industrialism, nationalism and higher education evolved over the years, its basic structure remained unchanged through the end of World War II.

This entire system is now unraveling. Nation-states are still powerful, but the era of their domination is rapidly coming to an end. Unyielding forces of globalization are creating new types of social, political and economic organization that require the formation of new institutions in every sector and at every level of society. As nation-states become increasingly entangled in a growing number of transnational networks of exchange, boundaries that have long seemed secure become permeable, and walls that have appeared to be solid begin to crumble. Just as the modern university was created at the moment of transition from an agricultural to an industrial economy, so what might be called the postmodern university must be created to negotiate the shift from industrial and consumer capitalism to financial capitalism and a network-driven world. Our most immediate concerns might be local, statewide or even national, but the most pressing long-term problems we face are international and global.

Parochial interests must be set aside to create global educational networks that will facilitate the production of new knowledge and encourage the free flow of intellectual and cultural capital. While the shape of these new institutions is far from clear, their general contours are beginning to emerge.

We can trace the history of our current crisis first to the turmoil of the 1960s and then deeper to developments in Europe at the end of the eighteenth century. All too often debates about the critical issues of our time are conducted in a historical vacuum. During the 1960s, developments within and beyond ivied walls created unprecedented unrest on campuses. The end of the postwar expansion of colleges and universities and the changing demographics of the student population collided with national and international events to create a volatile environment in which students demanded sweeping changes that faculty members and administrators were unable or unwilling to make. These conflicts, which often turned violent, created a crisis of authority and legitimization from which the academy has never recovered. The turmoil of the sixties led to the culture wars of later decades that still shape our social and political landscape. The seeds of conflicts surrounding what was later dubbed "political correctness" were sown during the 1960s and 1970s. Though many of these controversies began on college and university campuses, they had a considerably broader social and political impact.

It is important to recall that as far back as the administration of Richard Nixon, higher education has been a favorite target of conservative politicians and pundits.

Tensions within colleges and universities did not immediately lead to changes. One of the primary reasons faculty members and administrators could not or would not respond to the demands for change was their abiding commitment to a model of the university that was first defined by Immanuel Kant, a lonely eighteenth-century philosopher who never left his hometown in what was then Prussia and is today Russia. While medieval universities were intended to serve the needs of the church, Kant's plan for the modern university, which he published in 1798, was designed to serve the needs of emerging nation-states. He defined the structure of knowledge in higher education, carving it into divisions and departments that were suited to the time in which he lived. This plan was first implemented in 1810 at Humboldt University in Berlin and later imported to America at Johns Hopkins University in 1876.

For Kant, the university was to serve two primary functions: first, to provide educated bureaucrats for the state, and second, to conduct research whose goal was the production of new knowledge. In this scheme, teaching is relegated to so-called gymnasiums, educational institutions similar to advanced high schools. The disciplinary structure and division of responsibilities that Kant established have proven remarkably stable over the years, but the expansion of knowledge and

increasing complexity of problems created by the proliferation of information and the emergence of new areas
of inquiry can no longer be confined within traditional
disciplinary boundaries. It is, therefore, time to reassess
the effectiveness of this model.

But history alone does not explain the context for the
changes that are required. It is also necessary to examine
the social, political and economic significance of the
technological developments now occurring. During the
latter half of the twentieth century, we moved from what
can best be described as a world of walls and grids
(industrial factories and assembly lines) to a world of
networks (communications media and information-
processing devices linked in worldwide wireless webs).
Grids are closed—walls separate and isolate their components into autonomous regions, departments and
divisions; networks are open—webs connect and inter-
relate ideas, individuals and organizations. An understanding of how networks operate prepares the way for
reconceiving what universities should do and how they
should do it.

The same technologies that create opportunities for
productive change sometimes turn destructive. The
recent tumult in financial markets that led to a worldwide economic meltdown was made possible, perhaps inevitable, by new information, communications,
media and technologies. It has become commonplace
to insist that since the 1980s we have been living in a
bubble economy—junk bond bubble, dot-com bubble,
housing bubble, debt bubble. Now, as I said earlier, we

are facing the education bubble. Continuing problems in global financial networks are already having a profound effect on higher education, and this situation will worsen in the near future. Wealthy colleges and universities will survive and, in some cases, merge with other institutions, thereby becoming even more influential. Other colleges and universities will be taken over by foreign countries or organizations eager to expand their share of the growing education market or to jump-start their own education industry. Still others will be bought by for-profit businesses and redesigned to produce steady revenue streams. And, finally, many colleges and universities will simply close.

The changes I am going to propose are closely interrelated and are designed to both accommodate and take advantage of developments occurring in the broader society and culture. To reform the university system, we must begin by understanding the restructuring of knowledge now occurring. The organization of knowledge is neither set in stone nor hardwired in the brain, but changes as societies evolve and knowledge expands. Technological innovation alters the structure of knowledge, and, conversely, the changing structure of knowledge results in new technologies that transform both what we know and how we learn. Consider, for example, the difference between a traditional book like the one you are reading and the multimedia works, interactive websites and social networks so frequented by young people today. New ways of producing and communicating knowledge are forging different relationships among people that are transforming traditional academic disciplines in ways that we are just beginning to understand. When the organization of knowledge changes, the structure of educational institutions must be transformed. I will outline specific suggestions for institutional restructuring and spell out the implications of this plan for research, publication and teaching. I will also directly address the impact of these changes on the extremely contentious issues of mandatory retirement and tenure.

While many professional schools and vocational programs are doing a good job preparing students for viable professions and careers, most graduate programs in the arts, humanities and many of the social sciences are far less successful. Many of the skills cultivated in graduate programs and passed on to undergraduates are of diminishing value. It is, of course, essential for young people to learn how to read carefully, write effectively and think critically. But reading, writing and critical thinking, like knowledge itself, change with the times. With the development of sophisticated digital technologies, the resources for writing expand beyond the printed word to include animated images, sounds and graphic designs that allow for creative interaction between producers and consumers. As these resources spread, it is important to assess thoughtfully their advantages and disadvantages.

The insistence on narrow research and formats like traditional doctoral dissertations and heavily footnoted scholarly articles unnecessarily limits the creative possibilities for writing and critical thinking. While many professors are serious scholars and dedicated mentors, too often they are afraid of experimentation and change and fall back on the familiar past, making education a process of self-replication, insisting that students do exactly what has "always" been done. The past must give way to a future in which there is ample opportunity for collaborative interaction at every level of the education process. Teachers have much to offer their students, but students also have much to teach their teachers. Over the years, many of my undergraduate students have introduced me to new ways of writing and teaching that digital technologies make possible. Faculty members should work with undergraduate and graduate students to develop additional opportunities for creative expression fostered by new media.

This long and difficult process of reform will not succeed if we do not acknowledge how variegated the landscape of higher education is today. There has been much discussion about the social consequences of the increasingly inequitable distribution of wealth. What goes unnoticed in these debates is that capital is intellectual and cultural as well as financial. The story of higher education in America is a tale of two worlds: wealthy elite schools and poor public and private schools. The challenges faculty members, staff and administrators face in these two worlds are inverse mirror images of each other and, thus, one solution will not fit all institutions. If education is as important to our future as most people believe it is, we must find a way to bridge this gap by developing programs to redistribute intellectual and cultural capital. This will require new government programs designed to foster cooperation among the haves and have-nots in higher education. If the government can afford to bail out large corporations, big banks and financial institutions, it can afford to assist struggling colleges and universities.

I have learned over the years that if significant changes are to occur, they must begin modestly and grow widely. Any effective transformational strategy will have to be both bottom-up and top-down. In many ways, what is needed might begin most easily at the undergraduate level, where there is sometimes more flexibility and less disciplinary rigidity. But graduate programs at major research universities train tomorrow's teachers and set the professional standards by which they will be judged. It is, therefore, also important to begin the difficult process of transforming centuries-old traditions that still govern the upper levels of higher education. In order to suggest the kind of tactics that can be used to initiate change, I will offer examples of some of the initiatives I launched during my years at Williams College as well as the way in which we are redesigning the graduate program in the Study of Religion at Columbia University.

While some of the structural and substantive changes I propose are modest and local, others are radical and global. All of them, however, require a fundamental transformation of our vision of the world and, correlatively, a change in the values that inform individual decisions and institutional direction. Over a century ago, Friedrich Nietzsche wrote, "All things are entwined, enmeshed, enamored." We might translate Nietzsche's insight into today's terms by insisting that in the World Wide Web and Internet, everything is interconnected. Our growing interdependence creates enormous challenges and great opportunities for higher education. The best way to strengthen our colleges and universities is to create ways to make them more adaptive to our rapidly changing world and to develop effective strategies for making higher education affordable and accessible to more people across the globe.

2

Beginning of the End

On June 9, 1968, the day after Robert Kennedy was buried in Arlington National Cemetery, I graduated from Wesleyan University. Under the ominous clouds of a gathering thunderstorm, the world into which we were sent that morning seemed dangerously fragile. The Wesleyan I was leaving that day was very different from the university I had entered in the fall of 1964. I had grown up in a prosperous, staunchly Republican New Jersey suburb, the son of a father who was a high school science teacher and a mother who taught American literature in the public high school I attended. The school that awaited me that fall was all male, lily-white and firmly committed to the venerable tradition of liberal learning. Fraternities dominated campus social life, and women were allowed in the dorm rooms for only a few hours on weekend evenings. The only drug available was alcohol and there was plenty of it. By the spring of my senior year, the massive turmoil caused by social unrest and the resistance to the war in Vietnam crashed through the walls that had long separated the university from the rest of society and left nothing unchanged. It was a confusing time for young people who were trying to plot their future. The social and political events spinning out of control shattered all sense of certainty and security. Leaders in positions of authority ranging from parents and politicians to college and university professors and administrators were struggling with their moral compass.

Even as that fatal year of 1968 fades from memory, its ramifications continue to be felt. For adults who had suffered years of war and depression, the new generation seemed to be inhabiting a remarkably prosperous time, their lives privileged. While restless students had more and wanted for less than had been imaginable for their parents, many remained haunted by the uncertainty accompanying the prospect of nuclear destruction and were plagued by the suspicion that material well-being could not ensure happiness. As the currents unleashed by the sexual revolution, the civil rights movement and the antiwar movement intersected, the world rapidly became chaotic, and some major shifts seemed about to occur. The impact of these events was made much more immediate by television. When the Beatles appeared on *The Ed Sullivan Show* in February 1964, they did not so much trigger a social upheaval as represent the social and cultural revolution already well under way. As the postwar student population exploded, many universities expanded exponentially. Students and faculty members drifted farther and farther apart, and the educational process became increasingly impersonal. With images of American race riots and smoldering cities, as well as burning Asian villages and body bags returning from a war in a distant land, flashing across television screens, students became disaffected and found little "relevance" in the work their teachers were asking them to do. The student protests that spread across the country represented a complex mixture of self-interest and genuine idealism.

There is no doubt that the urgency of the social protest in the middle and late sixties was inspired by the threat of the military draft for privileged college students. But it would be a mistake to overlook other motivations. I was fortunate to have several professors who insisted on a close relationship between the abstract philosophical and religious ideas we were exploring in the classroom and the concrete social and political events going on beyond the confines of the university. The professor who was responsible for my majoring in religion, John Maguire, introduced me to Dr. Martin Luther King Jr. and helped me understand the stakes of the movement he led. One of my most vivid undergraduate memories was hearing King recite words from the Book of Amos while he was preaching in the Wesleyan chapel:

> Let justice roll on like a river
> And righteousness like an ever-flowing stream.
> (5:24)

These words still echo in my ears, and I try to pass on to my students the most valuable lessons my professors taught me. Many young people at the time shared King's dream of a more just world in which all people would have the opportunity for a good education and a better life; indeed, some of us still do.

Important disagreements notwithstanding, most young people on the left were convinced that critical political and economic decisions in the United States were made to advance the interests of what President Eisenhower had presciently dubbed the military-industrial complex. While often overstated, student concerns were not completely unfounded. During the Cold War, to conduct research and educate students many universities received lucrative grants and contracts from government agencies, the Department of Defense and even the CIA. William J. (Wild Bill) Donovan, who, we have recently learned, directed the espionage career of Julia Child at the Office of Strategic Services during World War II, also asked James Phinney Baxter III, president of Williams College, to help him recruit the best and brightest undergraduates. The secrecy of much of this work increased the suspicions and raised the level of paranoia among restive students. Most of the government money was funneled to the natural sciences, but some went to programs in the social sciences, including anthropology, sociology and history, as well as to fields of the humanities such as literature and languages. The government backed existing departments and disciplines but also supported the development of new programs aimed at addressing the threat posed by the Soviet Union and China. Initially funded privately by the Ford, Rockefeller and Carnegie foundations, these new fields of inquiry were designed to meet the needs of the government and the military. One year after the Soviet Union launched *Sputnik,* the federal government passed the National Defense Education Act (1958). This initiative was designed to improve young people's math, science and language skills and to create a pool of experts with substantial knowledge about areas of the world that were likely to become trouble spots. As the war in Vietnam heated up and draft deferments were revoked, these programs became lightning rods for student protests. Since students tended to be less aware of government involvement in some of the social sciences and humanities, they focused their protests on the hard sciences and research devoted to military technology. In the post–Cold War era, it is difficult to recall that some of America's most gifted students actually blew up buildings to bring an end to what they considered American imperialism and start a revolution inspired by Marx, Lenin, Mao, Fidel and Che.

Students were right when they claimed they were starting a world revolution, but were wrong about what revolution was then being launched. While rebelling against the military-industrial complex, they did not realize that media, digital and network technologies initially developed for military purposes would create another major revolution during the latter decades of the twentieth century. While the development and extensive distribution of personal computers marked an important milestone, the world did not significantly change until computers were linked together to create what can best be described as network culture, in which people across the globe are connected to one another. These networks, initially local and proprietary, quickly spread from universities and private businesses to encompass the entire world. Rapid developments over the past several decades tend to obscure the importance of changes that took place during the late 1960s. In his informative book *1968: The Year That Rocked the World*, Mark Kurlansky writes:

> There has never been a year like 1968, and it is unlikely that there will ever be one again. At a time when nations and cultures were separate and very different—and in 1968 Poland, France, the United States, and Mexico were more different from one another than they are today—there occurred a spontaneous combustion of rebellious spirits. . . .
>
> Four historic factors merged to create 1968: the example of the civil rights movement, which at the time was so new and original; a generation that felt so different and so alienated that it rejected all forms of authority; a war that was hated so universally around the world that it provided a cause for all the rebels seeking one; and all of this occurring at the moment that television was coming of age but was still new enough not to have yet become controlled, distilled, and packaged the way it is today. In 1968, the phenomenon of a same-day broadcast from another

part of the world was in itself a gripping new technological wonder.

A few weeks after the Beatles' appearance on *The Ed Sullivan Show,* Marshall McLuhan, who became famous for coining the phrase "global village," published a book that would prove prophetic—*Understanding Media: The Extensions of Man.* What McLuhan theorized, young people were living. While the Internet and the World Wide Web were still several decades away, May 1968 was the first tremor of what eventually would become the network revolution that would transform countries as distant as Russia, China and Iran. The global student revolution foreshadowed how increasing connectivity and speed of communication would transform the dynamics of social, political, economic and educational systems. May 1968 was neither planned nor organized but erupted spontaneously and simultaneously at multiple sites distributed throughout the world and spread at an increasing rate of speed as it moved across the globe.

Turmoil on college and university campuses deepened as a result of changes in the student population during the 1960s. When I entered Wesleyan in the fall of 1964, there were two African Americans in my class of 350; by the time I graduated four years later, 5 percent of the student body was African American. In the years that followed, students from diverse racial, ethnic and economic groups entered higher education in much larger numbers than ever before, and a growing number of women chose to pursue postsecondary study. With greater affluence and more affordable transportation, foreign study expanded, becoming a rite of passage for many American students, and young people in foreign countries found the lure of American colleges and universities irresistible.

As demographics shifted, student interests and demands began to change. A curriculum made up of works largely written by dead white men taught by tenured professors who were almost exclusively white men no longer seemed adequate. A diverse student body not unreasonably wanted a diverse curriculum. Young people demanded change that faculty members and administrators were either unable or unwilling to deliver. Faculty resistance provoked further student reaction, creating a self-reinforcing loop of accusation and recrimination. Already suspicious of authority, students began to demand that their teachers defend the books they assigned as well as their pedagogical practices. With chaos in the streets and tensions in the classroom, the university was no longer so removed from events in the real world.

Change was slow, but by the late 1970s and early 1980s, many of the undergraduates from the 1960s had received PhDs and were slowly infiltrating classrooms. Affirmative action and diversity initiatives transformed faculties in ways that should have been predictable but many educators and administrators found surprising. Young faculty members started to implement the changes their teachers had refused to make. Strategically

32

cunning, they took over programs such as Asian Studies, Soviet Studies and Middle Eastern Studies and turned them to their own ends. As the number of younger faculty members slowly increased, their ambitions grew, and new programs reflecting the changing faces of both the faculty and the student body emerged.

New faculty and different students, however, were not content with creating supplementary programs; they were determined to rewrite the traditional curriculum. By the mid-1980s, heated debates about what was described as the Western canon broke out within the academy and eventually attracted media interest that brought the controversy to the attention of the wider public. One side argued that the traditional curriculum was Eurocentric and represented the interests of powerful white middle-class and upper-middle-class men who saw their mission in life as the extension and protection of the American empire. From this point of view, the canon had to be either overthrown or revised to include individuals and groups who had been marginalized far too long. The other side countered that this criticism of the Western tradition was an assault on the very beliefs and values that had made America great. What was needed, they argued, was adherence to the tradition and more rather than less study of dead white men and their achievements. This academic debate launched the culture wars, which two decades later still divide the country.

The reaction to the changes on college and university campuses intersected with another current circulating just beneath the noise generated by sex, drugs and rock and roll. The personal promiscuity and social unrest created by the youth culture provoked calls for a return to traditional family, religion and values. In their campaign for inclusiveness, so-called tenured radicals consistently overlooked one important and growing minority—religious, social and intellectual conservatives. While committed to an ideology of difference, the leadership on most college and university campuses was not then and is not today politically and ideologically diverse. In some ways, campus liberals did conservatives a favor by excluding them. Left to their own devices, conservatives created alternative institutions like the American Enterprise Institute, the Cato Institute, the Heritage Foundation and the Manhattan Institute, which support research and underwrite a broad range of policy initiatives. More media savvy than their liberal counterparts, these conservatives launched important publication programs and sophisticated media projects designed to advance their political agenda by shaping public opinion.

The flames of the burgeoning culture wars were fanned by one of the most unlikely best sellers of all time—Allan Bloom's *The Closing of the American Mind: How Higher Education Has Failed Democracy and Impoverished the Souls of Today's Students.* Though laden with lengthy discussions of dense Greek and German philosophy, Bloom's 1987 book became a sensation that ignited a national debate about higher education in the United States. The book sold nearly half a million copies in hardback and was number one on the *New York Times* nonfiction best-seller list for four months. At the time of the book's publication, Bloom was a little-known professor in the Committee on Social Thought at the University of Chicago. *The Closing of the American Mind*, written at the urging of Bloom's friend and colleague Saul Bellow, was intended as a philosophical critique of the intellectual substance, or what he regarded as the lack of substance, of college and university curricula, the leftist political leanings of most faculty members and the pernicious effect of what he regarded as the lax morals and sexual excesses of students. Appearing during a time of growing social and political conservatism and economic distress, the book struck a deep nerve across the country.

Bloom announced what he saw as the most pressing problem in the first sentence of the book. He began, "There is one thing a professor can be absolutely certain of: almost every student entering the university believes, or says he believes, that truth is relative." This commitment to relativity in the name of democratic equality, Bloom argued, was the result of the permissiveness ushered in by the cultural and sexual revolution that began in the 1960s. Sounding an alarm calculated to provoke, Bloom repeatedly drew parallels between America in the late twentieth century and the conditions in Germany during the Weimar Republic that allowed Nazism to take root. He declared that the infatuation with popular culture and growing multiculturalism on campuses had led to an intellectual and moral breakdown that threatened the very fabric of American democracy. Far from addressing urgent social and political problems directly, Bloom, who was an unapologetic elitist, argued that misguided faculty members made matters worse by preaching the gospel of relativism and encouraging and promoting immoderate hedonism. "The students' wandering and wayward energies finally found a political outlet," Bloom wrote. "By the mid-sixties universities were offering them every concession other than education, but appeasement failed and soon the whole experiment in excellence was washed away, leaving not a trace. The various liberations [e.g., women's liberation and the movements for African American, Latin American and gay and lesbian rights] wasted that marvelous energy and tension, leaving students' souls exhausted and flaccid, capable of calculating, but not of passionate insight." For America to recover its greatness, he said, young people must turn away from the culture of permissiveness, excess and difference, and colleges and universities must return to their proper responsibility of teaching the great books of the Western tradition.

The Closing of the American Mind is an odd mix of scholarly analysis and political manifesto. Its pages are filled with fighting words, and fights broke out. The book was widely praised by conservative commentators, but liberal voices within and beyond the academy vehemently attacked Bloom and his argument. Writing in *The Times Literary Supplement,* David Rieff proclaimed Bloom to be "an academic version of Oliver North: vengeful, reactionary, antidemocratic." His book, Rieff continued, "is one that decent people would be ashamed of having written." But Bloom's ideas quickly began to circulate through the conservative corridors of power in Washington. Several of his students went on to play important roles in policy and political debates. Francis Fukuyama, the author of the widely influential book *The End of History,* and Paul Wolfowitz and Richard Perle, who would hold important positions in the administration of George W. Bush, were all his students.

Bloom's analysis exposed the widening fault lines between the university and society at large as well as the growing divisions within the university. His book appeared the same year the stock market crashed. While the nonacademic world always harbors suspicions about what goes on behind closed college and university doors, tensions seem to increase during times of economic hardship. In 1987, as in our own time, growing uncertainty about financial security led to increasing impatience with an educational system whose practical benefits were not clear. Bloom's insistence that the excesses of faculty members still high on the sixties led to a decline in moral and cultural values made higher education an easy target for critics. But with the economic turnaround and the dot-com boom of the 1990s, these concerns seemed less pressing. The problems that began brewing in the 1960s, however, did not go away. When Bloom's students became leading figures in neo-conservative political circles, the ideas he championed became very influential.

A divisive conflict of the culture wars of the 1980s, the one between senior tenured faculty members on the one hand and, on the other hand, junior nontenured faculty members and young graduate students, had been simmering for several decades. More diverse young people brought with them interests and values—including those shaped by the sixties—that differed from those of their older colleagues. But more important, because of an economic downturn in 1970, many jobs in higher education disappeared. The issue of employment, which has, of course, always been a major concern for young people considering graduate school, suddenly became urgent. I clearly remember sitting in John Maguire's office a few days after Martin Luther King Jr. had been assassinated, discussing my future. I had decided to pursue a doctorate and was considering three schools. My professor, whom I trusted completely, counseled, "It doesn't matter what you decide. They are all good programs. Get your degree and you'll have more job offers than you know what to do with." When I went on the job market in the fall of 1972, there were only three jobs in modern Western religion, which is one of the broadest possible areas of expertise, in the entire country. The situation has not improved significantly since then.

I have often wondered why nobody saw the collapse of the job market coming. Looking back, some of the reasons for the downturn are obvious. The end of the post–World War II expansion of colleges and universities led to a decline in the demand for new PhDs. Having grown too quickly during the sixties, schools had young tenured faculty members who weren't going anywhere for a long time; indeed, some of these people are still teaching. In addition, the continuing war in Vietnam and the mounting expense of President Johnson's Great Society programs combined to create pressures throughout the economy. When the oil crisis hit in the early 1970s, it was the last straw for overextended college and university budgets. Presidents turned down the thermostats, told everybody to put on an extra sweater and stopped hiring.

But not all aspects of the academic economy conformed to market principles. Even though the demand for PhD graduates dried up, the supply did not adjust to the new realities. After a decline from 1975 to 1985, the number of PhDs granted began increasing until it returned to the early 1970s level, a decade later.

Universities supported this irresponsible policy because they could not afford to cut back on graduate students—they had created a system in which this cheap labor was needed to teach undergraduates and do research in the labs of tenured faculty members. The job situation varied from field to field; it was best in some of the natural and social sciences and worst in the arts and humanities. But overall, the situation was daunting; even the graduates of the best programs in the country often could not find jobs.

Faced with escalating financial problems, universities sought new revenue streams, and graduate students developed strategies to defer the inevitable. In the late 1960s, some universities and private foundations be-

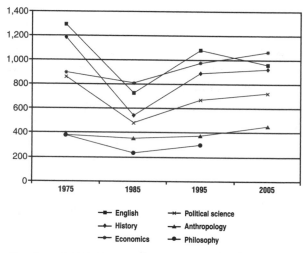

Number of PhD Degrees Given in Selected Disciplines

Reprinted by permission of the publisher from *How Professors Think: Inside the Curious World of Academic Judgment* by Michèle Lamont, p. 60. Cambridge, Mass.: Harvard University Press, copyright © 2009 by the President and Fellows of Harvard College.

came concerned about the length of time graduate students were taking to complete their doctorates. In an effort to expedite this process, they created incentives to get students in and out of doctoral programs in five years. When the economic crisis of the early 1970s hit, many schools began to rethink these initiatives and reverse course. Instead of helping students finish their work quickly, many universities required candidates to complete a master's degree *before* starting their doctoral work. This practice, which still continues, increased both the cost and the length of graduate education. In many cases, universities do not give fellowships for master's programs and instead use the income they generate to fund other parts of their operations. At Columbia, the only discretionary fund I have as chair of the religion department comes from the fees master's students pay. Students are still forced to assume more and more debt to complete their education.

With jobs scarce, students themselves began delaying the completion of their graduate work. Over my career, the time required for students to finish their graduate work has increased from five or six years to eight or nine years. Many of these students have spent two years getting a master's degree before they begin their doctoral program. Increasingly, the majority of these bright and dedicated young men and women have been unable to find positions in colleges and universities. Nationally, from 1975 to 1987, the median time taken to finish a PhD in the humanities went from 9.6 to 12 years. While doctoral students, unlike master's students, receive some financial support, it usually lasts only four or five years, and they are often forced to take part-time jobs or borrow yet more money to support themselves and, in many cases, their families. In addition, postdoctoral fellowships supposedly designed to alleviate the worsening job situation actually exacerbate the problem for graduate students. The practice of spending one to three years conducting additional research after receiving a PhD had been common in the natural sciences for years, but in the 1990s, people in the humanities also began pursuing postdocs. Though claiming that these programs serve the needs of students, universities also benefit by securing the services of the best and the brightest young people for assistance with research in the labs of their mentors and teaching courses that tenured faculty try to avoid. All of this costs relatively little and requires no long-term commitment by employers. To see how bad the situation has become, consider one of the most prestigious postdoctoral fellowships in the humanities: the Society of Fellows at Columbia. In the past four years, applications have increased from three hundred to one thousand for three to four places. This is a direct result of the deteriorating job market. Having been on the selection committee, I can say that many of these young scholars are extremely intelligent and very well qualified for faculty appointments; most of them, however, will never find an academic job. That is a tragic situation.

The world of graduate education obviously has changed considerably from that spring day in 1968 when I sat in my professor's office considering my future. Though my parents didn't have much money, they started saving what little they could for my college education the day I was born. I worked in the summers and during my years at Wesleyan to help with finances. A five-year fellowship at Harvard enabled me to graduate without debt and begin teaching at Williams College at the age of twenty-seven. My salary in 1973 was $10,000, and I was given a $500 summer research stipend, which, the department chair explained, was not part of my salary, so the college would not have to pay benefits on it.

Today my course would be quite different. I would

take a year off before beginning a master's program, which would require two years. Then I would start a doctoral program, which would take seven or eight years to complete. After that, if I were one of the fortunate few, I would spend three years in a postdoctoral program. During this time, my debt probably would be increasing; it surely would not be decreasing. At the end of this long process, I would begin looking for a job. If no tenure-track position materialized, I would spend three years in a series of one-year replacement jobs or would be forced to accept an adjunct position in which I would be paid between $1,000 and $5,000 per course and have no benefits. This protracted period of under-employment would come during what should be the most productive and creative years of a young person's career.

Unfortunately, this long and difficult apprenticeship frequently ends in failure. One of the dirty secrets of higher education is that only 35 percent of college and university positions are tenure or tenure-track. The remaining 65 percent of the workforce in higher education is made up of part-time adjuncts and teaching assistants, who are graduate students. If, at the end of this long process, I found myself in the unlikely position of having secured a rare tenure-track job, I would be in my late thirties, possibly with a wife and family, and tens of thousands of dollars in debt. My starting salary would be $55,000. If I did not get a job, I would take out another $150,000 in student loans and start law school. This story is not fanciful; I have seen it many times with former students, friends and colleagues. Those experiences are extremely frustrating for teachers as well as students and, from my point of view, raise serious ethical questions about encouraging young people to pursue graduate work in many fields.

As the number of jobs decreased, the demands for research and publication increased. With more and more people applying for fewer and fewer positions, faculty members and administrators making decisions needed new ways to distinguish among candidates. Research and publication came to play a much larger role in hiring and promotion decisions than in the past. Many schools never known for research, and faculty members who had published little or nothing, suddenly started asking young people to do what they themselves had never done. This increased demand for research and publication was part of a larger trend toward specialization in colleges and universities. But other factors were also at work.

Little attention has been paid to the importance for the academic world of the post–World War II transportation revolution. The globalization of higher education did not begin with the Internet but with airplanes. Over the past four decades, national and international seminars, symposia, colloquia and conferences have come to play a major role in the personal and professional lives of many globe-trotting faculty members. Prior to the mid-1960s, most academic meetings were local or at best regional affairs; faculty members attending drove or took buses and trains. Everything changed with the advent of cheap air travel. Faculty members were now jetting all over the world to meet with colleagues who shared their interests. With this development, new professional organizations and societies were established and new global networks emerged. The proliferation of these organizations actually narrowed the focus of research programs, and so-called cutting-edge work became more and more about less and less. These developments led to the further fragmentation of universities that were already riven by the recent diversification of the student body and faculty and the corresponding pluralization of curricula.

In an effort to attract members and raise money, professional societies sought to differentiate themselves from one another by restricting the focus of their activities. As new fields and programs were introduced, old departments began dividing themselves into ever narrower subfields. In a quest for recognition and academic legitimacy, each subfield established a professional organization to promote the interests of its members. As the fields of expertise became more restricted, the research of scholars working in them became more homogeneous, and communication among scholars with different concerns became less common. While claiming to embrace new methods that opened new lines of inquiry, too many academics took measures to protect their self-interest by policing their disciplinary borders and punishing those who crossed them.

In the new world of higher education that emerged in the latter half of the twentieth century, professional societies and international conferences were not enough to secure academic credibility. Publication became the currency of the realm.* Each professional society inaugurated a publication program that included journals and often book series on very narrow subjects. University presses followed suit by sponsoring a growing number of series on specialized topics. As the focus of these series narrowed, the potential market for books contracted. When financial pressures forced universities to cut back or eliminate subsidies and made it necessary for libraries to become much more selective in their purchases, university presses had to recalibrate their publishing programs. With print runs of merely three hundred to four hundred copies and sales often considerably lower than that, the scholarly monograph has no future. The problems are as bad or worse for journal publication. As double-digit cuts in library budgets are projected and the cost of journals continues to skyrocket, the situation is fast approaching a tipping point. Without radical changes, academic publishing will collapse in the near future. With its demise, the long-

---

*I must confess that over the years, I contributed to these developments. In the late 1970s, I served as the director of research and publication for the American Academy of Religion and was instrumental in establishing Scholars' Press (since taken over by Oxford University), which published several series of scholarly works on religion. In addition, I edited various series at other presses— Religion and Postmodernism (University of Chicago Press), Intersections: Philosophy and Critical Theory (State University of New York Press) and Kierkegaard and Postmodernism (Florida State University Press).

standing system of evaluating individual faculty members and ranking institutions will unravel and new criteria and procedures for assessment will have to be developed.

Colleges and universities are more isolated from the world and inwardly fragmented today than ever before. But the roots of this antiquated structure run deep. Indeed, the overspecialized university is the logical development of the model Immanuel Kant defined in the late eighteenth century. Since we cannot solve a problem unless we know how it emerged, we must pause to consider the ghost of Kant still haunting the halls and classrooms of today's colleges and universities.

3

Back to the Future

As the cost of higher education continues to increase, many people are raising questions about the value of the liberal arts. When college and university professors are asked why liberal learning continues to be important, the most common response they offer is, "Because it promotes critical thinking." But what is "critical thinking"? The most concise answer to this question is: critical thinking is thinking about thinking. This response is easily misunderstood because it seems to suggest that education in the liberal arts turns away from the world and has little or no practical value. This is, admittedly, always a danger; indeed, some faculty members go so far as to insist that like art for art's sake, knowledge exists for knowledge's sake and should not be judged by its usefulness. This attitude, however, is both misleading and shortsighted. While critical thinking is not simply utilitarian, it does have very significant practical implications. By turning back on itself, thought examines the ways in which we make the judgments about truth, value and beauty without which civilized society is impossible. The liberal arts expose students to different ways of understanding the world and acting in it. Moreover, critical thinking cultivates the skills necessary for making responsible decisions that change the lives of individuals and transform the world. Such reflection has never been more important than in this era of media frenzy and information overload.

To appreciate the abiding importance of liberal education, it is helpful to consider the historical tradition in which it emerged. The lack of historical perspective is one of the most important factors blocking reforms that are so desperately needed. The story begins in 1798 in Immanuel Kant's small town in Prussia, where Kant was better known to his neighbors and local shopkeepers for the punctuality of his daily walks than for his transformative philosophical vision that marks the transition to the modern world. His philosophy, which has been dubbed critical philosophy, had redefined the nature of knowledge, recast the foundations of morality and religion, summed up the Enlightenment, framed the guiding principles of the French Revolution, and first proposed the definition of art that became normative for the entire history of modernism. Kant's interests were not merely theoretical; to the contrary, he always insisted that in some of its capacities reason must be guided by practical interests that have concrete implications for daily life in the real world.

The practical impact of Kant's abstract and often difficult philosophy has nowhere been more directly felt than in the history of the modern university. Kant lived during a period of enormous change, when the early stages of the industrial revolution were transforming the economy and creating great human suffering and social upheaval. These developments gave rise to doubts and uncertainties that called into question long-held beliefs and well-established institutions. It was also a time of widespread political turmoil throughout Europe. The ancien régime was collapsing, and the modern nation-state was taking shape.

Such rapid change had a significant impact on higher education. Prior to the modern period, the dominant model for the university throughout Europe was the medieval university. During the Dark Ages (ca. 476–999), learning throughout the West was confined to monasteries or schools associated with local cathedrals like Paris, Chartres, Rheims and Utrecht. The most important of these schools were under the direction of prominent teachers who exercised considerable influence in shaping the texts and traditions that were handed down to later generations. As the economy improved and society revived, the growing population migrated to rapidly expanding cities. During the Middle Ages (ca. 1000–1517), major universities were founded in leading European urban centers. With the shift from local schools to urban universities, education became more expansive and educators more cosmopolitan. However, there were limits, which in time became barriers to further development: medieval universities were closely associated with the church, and religious education as well as theological training formed an important part of their mission. But the world was changing; travel increased with the growth of commerce and trade and with repeated Christian crusades to recover the Holy Land, which had fallen into the hands of Islamic "infidels," and as Europeans ventured farther afield they came into contact with different cultures and intellectual traditions. These developments set in motion changes that eventually would bring about the end of the Middle Ages and lead to the modern world.

By the end of the eighteenth century, the medieval system of education was no longer functional. Educational institutions had to be transformed to meet new societal needs. Most important, nascent nation-states replaced the churches as patrons of higher education. When the source of funding shifted from church to state, the purpose of education changed. Universities struck a deal with states: in return for dependable funding, they would provide an educated workforce to fill positions in rapidly expanding administrative bureaucracies—civil servants, professionals and businessmen. A win-win system.

Kant recognized the far-reaching implications of the changes and in 1798 published a treatise entitled *The Conflict of the Faculties*, in which he provided the blueprint for the modern university. In his remarkably prescient opening paragraph, he applied the central principles of his overall philosophical vision to the structure of the university:

> Whoever it was that first hit on the notion of a university and proposed that a public institution of this kind be established, it was not a bad idea to

handle the entire content of learning (really, the thinkers devoted to it) by *mass production,* so to speak—by a division of labor, so that for every branch of the sciences there would be a public teacher or *professor* appointed as its trustee, and all of these together would form a kind of learned community called a *university* (or higher school). The university would have a certain autonomy (since only scholars can pass judgment on scholars as such) and accordingly it would be authorized to perform certain functions through its *faculties.*

The three pillars upon which the university rests, as Kant envisioned it, are the principle of autonomy or self-determination, the mechanical logic of industrialism, and the distinction between usefulness and uselessness. As we will see, these principles are still the foundation of higher education. All of them must be changed.

Recalling Adam Smith's account of the machinations of the market and anticipating the logic that would eventually give rise to the assembly lines that made industrial capitalism profitable, Kant argued that the university produces education for *mass consumption.* In order to function efficiently, the labor process must be divided into separate departments and subdepartments, each of which has different expertise, tasks and responsibilities. The educational product is packaged as individual courses that are discrete units with set values.

Each course is the same size or length and conforms to university-wide standards. In order to be certified by the university, students must pass through a preestablished program whose requirements are set by the faculty and administration. The most important aspect of Kant's organizational structure is the division between the "higher" faculties, which include theology, law and medicine, and the "lower" faculty, which is philosophical. The philosophical faculty includes all departments and programs in what we today call the arts and sciences.

The distinction between the higher faculties and lower faculty reflects Kant's lingering commitment to certain aspects of the medieval university and wariness of relying on government support. By distinguishing the responsibilities of professional schools from the faculty of arts and sciences, Kant created a source of conflict between faculties that still plagues universities. In contrast to independent academies, where there is research but no teaching, and the gymnasium (i.e., high school), where there is teaching but no research, the university is designed to combine research and teaching. Kant's description of members of the higher faculties is very important for the later history of the university:

> While only the scholar [i.e., member of the lower faculty] can provide the principles underlying their functions, it is enough that they [i.e., members of the higher faculties] retain empirical knowledge of the statutes relevant to their office

(hence what has to do with practice). Accordingly, they can be called the *businessmen* or technicians of learning. As tools of the government (clergymen, magistrates and physicians), they have legal influence on the public and form a special class of the intelligentsia, who are not free to make public use of their learning as they see fit, but are subject to the censorship of the faculties.

When Kant described students in theology, law and medicine as "businessmen or technicians of learning" who are "tools of the government," he chose his words very carefully. These phrases are not neutral but express a value judgment that has had a profound influence on the subsequent history of higher education. While Kant acknowledges the necessity for the university to serve the state by providing educated citizens, he clearly thinks the role the philosophical faculty plays is more important. Furthermore, he realizes that strings are always attached. In accepting money from the state, the university agrees to limit the freedom of expression of members of the higher faculties; indeed, they do not enjoy academic freedom, but are subject to government censorship and control.

In contrast to the practical orientation of the higher faculties, the lower faculty extends the tradition of otherworldliness characteristic of medieval monasteries and universities to modern educational institutions. The arts and sciences in the philosophical faculty are not bound by utilitarian principles, but are designed to be "autonomous." Never yielding to personal, religious, political or economic interests, members of the philosophical faculty are supposed to be guided solely by the principles of pure or universal reason, which is purportedly untainted by practical concerns. This claim points to a puzzling ambiguity in Kant's view of the university. Although he insists that theology, law and medicine are the higher faculties, he defines the primary responsibility of the lower philosophical faculty as sitting in judgment over them. The autonomy of the arts and sciences faculty enables it to fulfill its critical function *within* the university. For Kant, the purity of reason is a prerequisite for philosophy, and the dedication to it is necessary for the lower faculty to play its role in judging the higher faculties. Within this scheme, the raison d'être of the arts and sciences is *criticism*. For critics devoted to purportedly disinterested inquiry, nothing compromises the purity of the faculty more quickly than government interference and the crass calculations of "businessmen and technicians of learning."

The autonomy of the lower faculty is, however, fragile and is always in danger of falling prey to outside interests. And to repeat, in order to protect the autonomy necessary for critical judgment, Kant insists that the arts and sciences faculty, unlike the so-called higher faculties, must be granted academic freedom as well as protection from government intervention. This is a very important point whose far-reaching implications did not become apparent until 1915, when the American Association of University Professors instituted the practice of tenure, supposedly to protect academic freedom.

The independence from practical affairs, as I said,

is intended to enable faculty members to make disinterested or objective judgments. There is, however, a further consequence of Kant's principle of autonomy that is not immediately obvious. In explaining the implementation of the division of labor, he writes, "for every branch of the sciences there would be a public teacher or *professor* appointed as its trustee, and all of these together would form a kind of community called a *university*." And then, as noted earlier, he adds almost in passing, "The university would have a certain autonomy (since only scholars can pass judgment on scholars as such)." The multiple aspects of the principle of autonomy or self-determination not only create a gulf between the university and the real world but also erect barriers between and among different divisions and departments *within* the university.

While most faculty members today decry the deregulation of modern financial markets, they vehemently defend the two-hundred-year-old tradition of self-regulation according to which no one can tell them how to conduct their business. As a result of the principles Kant defined, the work done by faculty members can be judged only by other "experts" in the same field or subfield, thereby isolating departments from one another. There is not even an obligation to communicate the importance of one's work or the results of one's research to people in other departments and disciplines, to say nothing of the wider public. To the contrary, efforts to work across fields and to communicate beyond the confines of the university are regarded as unprofessional and thus discouraged.

This limited view of the responsibility of faculty members is also the basis of the practice of peer review, which eventually leads to the culture of expertise that creates overspecialization among faculty members who are more interested in pursuing their narrow research agendas than they are in teaching what students need to learn and addressing pressing practical issues. The combination of the principles of self-regulation and peer review creates a form of faculty governance that makes significant change very unlikely. This closed system has become dysfunctional; new methods of assessment and more open styles of governance must be developed. I will consider some alternatives to these policies and practices in due course.

Kant's related distinction between usefulness and uselessness has proven to be equally problematic for higher education. The contrast between knowledge that is practical and knowledge that is impractical leads to a series of oppositions that continue to define the structure of the university. Not only useful/useless, but: practical/critical, profitable/unprofitable, professional schools/arts and sciences. The conflict of the faculties in the title of Kant's essay refers to the clash of values between these faculties, which is still going on today. Within this scheme, professional schools privilege the former alternatives and the arts and sciences faculty values the latter.

These hierarchical oppositions also form the basis of the distinction between research and teaching, which creates further divisions in colleges and universities. As I have noted, Kant proposes independent academies, funded by the government, which are devoted exclusively to research, and gymnasia, in which faculty members teach but are not expected to conduct research. In universities, faculty members are expected both to engage in original research and to teach. But these two activities are not regarded equally; research and publication are consistently valued much more highly than teaching. The former are misleadingly represented as the production of knowledge, the latter its transmission. Those who can, conduct research and write, according to the old cliché; those who can't, teach. Unfortunately, this hierarchy still lies at the heart of today's research universities and reinforces the disrespect for teachers that plagues not only universities and colleges but also society as a whole.

It is important to note that the role of teaching differs significantly in colleges and universities. In colleges the evaluation of teaching by students and colleagues usually plays a significant role in the assessment of faculty members. In universities, by contrast, the emphasis on research and publication completely overshadows the quality of teaching. Though most universities pay lip service to teaching and rely on student course evaluations, in my experience, teaching ability plays no significant role in hiring and promotion decisions. Publications and the evaluations of other specialists in the field are virtually all that count. Furthermore, some universities actually disdain college faculty members. When I was considered for tenure at Columbia, the administration would not accept letters of evaluation from any faculty member who teaches at a college. Having devoted most of my professional life to undergraduate liberal arts education, I was puzzled by this practice and, when I asked for an explanation, was told that the reason for the exclusion was that college professors do not train graduate students. So much for the value of undergraduate education.

The implications of this vision of the university become clearer when we cast a glance in an unlikely direction—the history of modern art. Most people have heard about the idea of art for art's sake, but what few realize is that it was Kant who first formulated this idea in its modern form. What occurred in the art world at the end of the eighteenth century holds important lessons for what is happening in the world of higher education at the beginning of the twenty-first. Kant's analysis turns on the distinction between high or fine art and low art or craft. In developing his plan for the university, he gives high and low art reversed roles. While low art is produced for the market and is intended to be profitable, high art, which is critical, is created for its own sake and is deemed to be intrinsically valuable. With the extension of this principle, art for art's sake becomes knowledge for knowledge's sake.

This distinction between high and low art emerged for very practical reasons at the time Kant was writing. With the decline of aristocratic and ecclesiastical power and the emergence of the bourgeoisie brought by the advent of modern industrialism, the conditions of artistic production and consumption changed significantly. In a manner similar to what is happening now in higher education, medieval patronage collapsed and the artistic "tenure system" disappeared. With this unexpected turn of events, art was transformed into a commodity, and artists had to compete in the marketplace. Art no longer was produced exclusively for wealthy patrons who enjoyed leisure and were unburdened by the necessity to work, but now had to be marketed by effectively addressing consumers with different interests. The emergence of a market economy created the new class of the bourgeoisie, whose members were neither exactly producers (workers) nor nonproducers (aristocrats). Like today's parents on the Upper West Side trying to get their three-year-olds into the "best" preschool programs, members of this emerging class needed cultural markers by which to establish their status and social identity. The interests of artists and consumers intersected in the search for cultural artifacts that were not supposed to be completely subject to market forces. The creation and possession of works of art came to serve as a means of securing social distinction. For art to serve no practical function, however, it had to be clearly distinguished from all commodities that could have a utilitarian end. Art, in the strict sense of the term, became "high art" or "pure art," which was distinguished from crafts, mass art and popular art.

When the line between high and low is drawn in this way, it becomes clear that the conflict of the faculties involves two competing systems of value and economic logic. For the businessmen and technicians of learning, value and profitability are directly related to market forces (i.e., the more popular and profitable, the more valuable), and for intellectuals and artists, true value cannot be calculated by the market. To the contrary, value and utility or economic popularity and profitability are inversely related (i.e., the more popular and profitable, the less valuable). By the latter half of the twentieth century, the contrast between the useful or profitable and the useless or unprofitable had spread beyond the professional schools/arts and sciences divide to "taint" what once was believed to be the purity of the philosophical faculty. The persistence of this attitude still creates problems for students. On October 4, 2009, a few days after the unemployment rate in the United States hit 9.8 percent, Jennifer Williams published an article in *The New York Times* entitled "Hard Work, No Pay" reflecting on her experience as she looked for a job.

> In my master's program, we talked a lot about theory and personal vision. We could experiment with whatever we wanted and it was wonderful. We tried not to dwell on earthy, unpleasant topics like money, or how to make it.
>
> In the Peace Corps, I taught art as a vocational skill. "Artists," the headmistress at my school in Ghana told me in words that were less than prophetic, "can always make a living."
>
> If I were to make an artwork expressing this period of unemployment, I would make stacks and stacks of little box-shaped rooms wallpa-

pered with résumés. Each room would have one little person inside and one window. That is what I felt like. Boundless possibilities, but hemmed in by the walls of an apartment where I spent every day looking for a way to afford all the things I wanted to do.

The worst thing was the feeling of uselessness—the fear that I was simply unskilled and unable to compete. Where had I miscalculated when I was planning out my life?

More and more young people are asking the same question. And it's not just the walls of apartments that are hemming them in, but also walls within the universities and between universities and our daily existence.

And yet, many faculty members continue to insist that if education is practical or profitable it must be kitsch and should no more be included in university curricula than commercial art should be admitted to the sacred precincts of the museum. This point was driven home to me more than a decade ago. In the late 1990s, I cofounded a for-profit company, Global Education Network, whose mission was to provide high-quality online education to people of all ages throughout the world. We were concerned about the escalating cost of education and the growing financial pressures on colleges and universities. By using new communications technologies, we developed a strategy for increasing and diversifying educational opportunities at a lower cost, while at the same time generating a new revenue stream for colleges and universities as well as for faculty members in the arts and humanities. As we will see in a later chapter, the importance of finding additional sources of income beyond tuition has become urgent. We invited eight leading universities and four top colleges to join us in this venture, and all but one turned us down. Though we devoted considerable time, effort and financial resources to the venture, the company eventually failed. The reason universities and colleges declined to join us was that faculty members, primarily in the arts and humanities, refused to participate in a for-profit venture, even though their own institutions would be equity partners and they would have complete control over the content of the courses on the network. In meetings with representatives from colleges and universities, faculty members time after time declared that higher education should not be corrupted by money and therefore should not be involved with for-profit ventures. This point of view is as outdated as the patronage system on which it relied. Academics have yet to admit what artists learned over two hundred years ago—it is possible to pursue art for art's sake or knowledge for knowledge's sake only if someone else is paying the bills.

As I said earlier, Kant's plan was first implemented by Wilhelm von Humboldt at the University of Berlin, which was founded in 1810. Von Humboldt, a follower of Kant and close friend of many influential German philosophers and Romantic poets, was a distinguished linguist, philosopher, diplomat and educator. He is widely acknowledged as the architect of the Prussian educational system, which served as a model for countries from the United States to Japan. The University of Berlin was the crown jewel in von Humboldt's system. In words that clearly echo Kant's vision for the philosophical faculty, von Humboldt insisted that university study should be "unforced and non-purposeful." The goal of education is the pursuit of knowledge for knowledge's sake, which leads to the process of self-cultivation. The personal quest of self-discovery is, in effect, an internalization of the traditional grand tour or year abroad that has long been enjoyed by the privileged sons and, more recently, daughters of wealthy Europeans and Americans.

By following the model that Kant defined and von Humboldt implemented, universities throughout the world have attempted to combine research, teaching and professional training in a variety of ways. Even in countries with different traditions, where research institutions were slower to develop, these principles of organizational structure and educational mission exercised considerable influence on educational policy. In England, for example, Oxford and Cambridge established residential colleges in rural settings and a tutorial system for individual instruction. Education extended beyond the classroom and lecture hall to the playing field and personal life. Though subject to utilitarian pressures, which usually originated in Scotland, British universities like Oxford and Cambridge remained dedicated to ideals of self-cultivation and knowledge for knowledge's sake that are very similar to the principles promoted in Germany.

The history of higher education in the United States is, in large measure, the story of the struggle to combine the German university and the British college. The first American university was Harvard, which included among its founders several Oxford graduates and about thirty-five Puritans, who were graduates of Cambridge's Emmanuel College. Their firm commitment to the model of residential colleges with a strong emphasis on moral character development led the Puritans to harbor deep suspicions of education that had little practical purpose. For early pioneers—educational and otherwise—the aim of education was to train leaders for service in church, state and society. This practical orientation was reinforced by a profound sense of pragmatism that runs deep in the American grain. For many people who came to the New World, classical European education appeared to be antidemocratic and reflected aristocratic ideals from which they had fled. When universities strayed too far from principles of practicality, various legislative authorities often intervened. In 1850, for example, the Massachusetts General Court "called on Harvard to reform its curriculum in order to prepare 'better farmers, mechanics, or merchants.' " Half a century later, Theodore Roosevelt expressed a similar sentiment on the occasion of the dedication of a new law school building at the University of Chicago: "We need to produce, not genius, not brilliancy, but the homely, commonplace, elemental virtues." Such views did not, of course, go uncontested. At the same time as the Massachusetts court was issuing its edict, Henry Tappan, who would soon become the president of the University of

Michigan, complained: "We have cheapened education so as to place it within the reach of everyone." This concern reflects sentiments also expressed by Nathan Lord, president of Dartmouth from 1828 to 1863, when he insisted that college education was not intended for people who planned to "engage in mercantile, mechanical, or agricultural operations."

Eventually, workable compromises between contrasting views of higher education were reached. Though the British college has been very important for American higher education, the model of the German research university also played a significant role from the country's early days. In 1824, Thomas Jefferson, to the dismay of many of his critics, recruited faculty members from Germany and England to teach at the University of Virginia. The most important effect of German influence came in 1876, when Johns Hopkins used the proceeds from his Baltimore and Ohio Railway to create the first American university devoted to "pure scholarship." Initially, it appeared that universities would be committed primarily to original research and scholarship, while colleges would have the responsibility for teaching the history and tradition of different disciplines and passing on the results of work being done at universities. However, a mere two years after Hopkins's initiative, historian of higher education Frederick Rudolph points out, Charles William Eliot used the occasion of his inaugural address at Harvard to insist on the necessity of "purposefully obliterating or at least diffusing the lines between undergraduate and graduate, between collegiate and scholarly." The poles of debate have remained relatively constant ever since.

American higher education has consistently wrestled with the problem of balancing the practical and the impractical, the common and the elite, the applied and the theoretical. The challenge of teaching is not merely to convey information but also to encourage students to ask questions they never imagined asking. This is what it means to think critically. But asking such questions is not enough; it is also necessary for students to learn how to formulate a position and develop thoughtful arguments to defend it. As I have suggested, there are practical implications to the most theoretical inquiry, and therefore questions of value are unavoidable. An education that does not provide students with the knowledge, background and perspective to understand the practical impact of ideas and actions is woefully inadequate in the global society that is now emerging.

4

Emerging Network Culture

Recent history is no less important for higher education than more or less ancient history. Since the 1960s, the university and the broader society and culture have been moving in opposite directions. We have seen that contentious conflicts created by developments ranging from campus unrest in the sixties and the culture wars of the seventies to the identity politics and political correctness of the nineties raised barriers between colleges and universities and the world at large. At the same time, faculties and the student body were becoming more internally fragmented. As these divisions were growing and deepening, the world was becoming more interconnected. While aspects of recent social and cultural changes have been described as the transition from an industrial to a postindustrial economy or as the shift from modernism to postmodernism, what is occurring is best understood as the appearance of *network culture.*

Network culture is characterized by the emergence of a new information and communications infrastructure that has been developing since the 1970s. Most of these technologies were originally created with government support and intended for military purposes, but they quickly became commercialized and spread throughout society. The evolution of this infrastructure has been very rapid and continues at an accelerating rate. In the late 1960s and early 1970s, mainframe computers gave way to personal computers, which were then linked to form networks. With the recent introduction of handheld devices and wireless technology, these networks have become ubiquitous and their impact has increased exponentially.

The creation of the Internet and the World Wide Web has been the most significant development in network culture to date. In the early days of its emergence, the rights to the use of Internet technology were granted first to university and military contractors working on the project, and access was gradually extended more widely. By the early 1980s, the National Science Foundation (NSF) had established a network that enabled universities to communicate for purposes of research. Commercial networks started appearing at this time, but the NSF did not turn over control of the Internet to commercial interests until 1994. That same year saw another decisive development for network culture—the introduction of graphic interfaces and Web browsers like Mosaic, Netscape and eventually Internet Explorer, which made the World Wide Web much easier to use and created the prospect for completely unanticipated commercial applications. As these networks expanded, they were deregulated, and when the Internet was commercialized, companies quickly adapted. At this point, innovation shifted from the non-profit to the for-profit sector; colleges and universities were left struggling to catch up and had to pay exorbitant prices for what they had helped to originate.

It is important to recognize that the Internet is actually a network of networks and the World Wide Web is a web of webs. The range of networks now connecting us includes, among others, media, financial, phone, military, terror and social networks. This constantly changing infrastructure has already transformed news and entertainment media, financial markets, military operations and the sociopolitical order, engineering a shift from the local to the global far beyond what most people imagined possible a decade ago. In coming years, emerging network culture will have an increasingly important impact on colleges and universities. If we are to appreciate the scope of the changes that need to be made in higher education, it is necessary to consider the conditions that have led to our current situation and then to examine the distinctive structure and operation of new global networks.

The collapse of the Berlin Wall serves as an effective symbol of the turning point from a world of walls to a world of webs. Though rarely noted, there is a direct line connecting the social unrest that reached a boiling point in 1968 and the world-transforming events of 1989. During the middle of the twentieth century, the ideology of the Cold War formed the foundation of a world system that created stability in the midst of considerable tension by setting two clearly defined adversaries against each other. When the Berlin Wall fell, it was more the result of economic developments, technological change and the spread of media, popular culture and consumer capitalism than of a calculated military strategy. As new media and information systems became more widely available, walls that governments previously had been able to police became permeable, and change was unavoidable. Karl Marx famously declared that in industrial capitalism, those who control the means of production have the political and economic power to control society. In network culture, by contrast, those who control the means of the reproduction and dissemination of information are able to exercise political and economic power throughout society. The dynamics of power change when societies, nations and finally the world are wired. The distributed structure of information, media and financial networks tends to subvert centralized power and destabilize established authority.

When the story of the Internet and the World Wide Web is told, an important chapter invariably is overlooked. The same 1960s counterculture that despised the military, resisted the war in Vietnam, marched for civil rights and disrupted college and university classrooms played a critical role in creating the technological revolution that made the emergence of network culture and with it a new economic order all but inevitable. The distance separating Haight-Ashbury from Silicon Valley is not as great as it initially appears. Young people in the sixties were divided between those who were concerned with political transformation and those who were preoccupied with personal transformation. Both groups shared suspicions about the so-called System and were committed to social change. Where they differed was on how best to bring that change about. Political activists argued that to change minds, you must first change society; hippies countered that it is necessary to change consciousness to transform the world. Though neither side ever converted the other, they were able to join forces in the common cause of personal and social change. For those who directed their efforts to changing consciousness, computers eventually replaced drugs as the mind-altering agent of choice. Stewart Brand, onetime member of Ken Kesey's Merry Pranksters (whose band was the Grateful Dead), founder of the legendary *Whole Earth Catalog* and author of *The Media Lab: Inventing the Future at MIT,* makes this telling point clearly and concisely: "This generation swallowed computers, just like dope." Many early enthusiasts believed that personal computers, connected in ever-expanding networks, held the promise of creating a more humane world by bringing people from different cultural, racial, ethnic and religious backgrounds together. As information and knowledge spread, consciousness would be transformed and mutual understanding would grow. Intoxicated with more than PCs, these visionaries obviously overlooked the darker side of digital communication technologies. As people draw closer, differences become more obvious and conflict often erupts. The global village, after all, is not always a peaceful place.

One of the primary places where the counterculture morphed into cyberculture was the early popular website known as the WELL (Whole Earth 'Lectronic Link). On the WELL, writers, artists and freaks joined computer geeks from the San Francisco Bay's legendary Homebrew Computer Club to debate the social and political implications of personal computers. It was at a meeting of the Homebrew Club that Steve Wozniak first demonstrated what he and his erstwhile hippie friend Steve Jobs one day would launch as Apple Computer. Jobs, Wozniak and their buddies created the world in which today's students live. The iPhone and iPod are further extensions of the PC revolution. As networks become less centralized and more distributed, information and communications devices form the very ether without which life for many young people is impossible.

Networks, of course, are not new; before the Internet and World Wide Web, there were ship, train, automobile, postal, telegraph and telephone networks. All networks, however, are not the same. The distinctive characteristics of the networks that are important for reforming higher education today come into sharp relief when they are compared to network television, which began appearing in the 1950s. Although the first regular television station was established in 1940 and both CBS and NBC started commercial transmission in 1941, networks equipped for coast-to-coast broadcasts were not established until 1951. The history of television, like that of the Internet decades later, is inseparable from its use by the military. During World War II, the refinement of the cathode-ray tube, cameras, transmitters and receivers used in radar, oscillators and other devices led to a marked improvement in the quality of television. When these technological advances were made available for commercial use after the war, affordable TV sets quickly became widely available. With the emergence of national networks in the early 1950s, businesses had a new venue for mass advertising. As images and information began to circulate around the world faster than ever before, distance collapsed and boundaries slipped away. The impact of this development was not merely economic but also social, political and cultural.

And yet, for all its novelty, TV shares more with the industrial past than the networked future. From its earliest stages, network television has functioned as an extension of the mechanical means of reproduction typical of industrial and consumer capitalism. Nationwide advertising vastly expanded mass markets and led to growing standardization of products manufactured and consumed. While promising to give customers unprecedented choice, advertisers actually offered them a limited range of options. National and international marketing campaigns did not completely erase regional and personal differences, but the increasing uniformity of products and purchasing habits created greater social homogenization throughout the 1950s.

The uniformity of transmission tends to create a uniformity of response. Television is a broadcast medium that deploys a one-to-many distribution system. Like students passively listening to lectures in a classroom, people stare at screens and blankly absorb what is dished out to them. You can't talk back to TV; the only possible response is to either switch channels or turn it off. In addition to this limitation, television does not allow viewers in different locations to communicate about what they are watching in real time. Rather than connecting people, TV isolates the individual viewer in front of the separate set. Though recording devices for TV programs eventually were developed, the quality and ease of reproduction, storage and transmission are severely limited.

These old centralized broadcast networks differ from new decentralized networks in many ways that are important for how media and information are produced, communicated and consumed. To understand the implications of these differences for higher education, it is necessary to consider several additional characteristics of the new network infrastructure.

First, today's networks use digital rather than analog technology. While the details of analog and digital technologies need not concern us here, several aspects of the differences between them are important for understanding their respective limitations and capabilities for education. In traditional analog media like telephones and VCR tapes (and television for much of its history), the signal is continuous and cannot be divided without weakening it. As a result of this limitation, analog communication tends to be point-to-point, and bandwidth (i.e., the portion of the network needed to convey the signal) is allocated according to the location and capacity of the sender and receiver. In digital technology, the signal is divided into discrete bits that can be reproduced, divided and distributed without any loss in quality or strength. Transmission does not have to be point-to-point but can utilize the resources of the entire network, and bandwidth can be allocated according to the information load, which is much more efficient. These innovations make possible many-to-many communication that facilitates group exchanges in real time. When a verbal or audio message, image or video is sent across the Internet, it is broken up into packets that seek out different paths across the network, in search of the fastest way to their destinations, where they are reassembled. There are four primary advantages to digital over analog technology that are important in this context. First, digital networks can handle different media (i.e., words, images, audio and video) equally effectively; second, data can be transmitted without suffering degradation; third, synchronous multiparty communication is possible; and fourth, digital networks are much faster than analog. So when digital devices are deployed on the Internet and the World Wide Web, more people can be connected, and information in more kinds of media can be sent more quickly and effectively.

A second distinctive characteristic of decentralized digital networks is that they are interactive. These networks are not centralized hierarchical structures in which the sender is active (i.e., a producer) and the recipients are passive (i.e., consumers); rather, they facilitate free exchange in which everybody can be both active and passive and, thus, participate both as a producer and as a consumer.

In terms of traditional pedagogical practices, centralized broadcast networks resemble the lecture format and decentralized interactive networks simulate a seminar arrangement. It is important to stress that distributed networks facilitate exchange not only between instructor and student but also among students themselves. In my experience, online class exchanges tend to generate additional discussion groups and forums, which often expand beyond the members of the class. Obviously, such interactivity is not limited by physical proximity but can occur among all people who have access to the necessary technology. Several of my courses have led to international discussion groups with students from the United States, Europe and Australia. The possibilities for interaction extend from individuals to institutions. As we will see below, online teleconferencing technology opens new possibilities for cooperation among colleges and universities as well as other institutions and organizations throughout the world.

Third, interactivity promotes diversity and increases both the freedom and the responsibility of members on the network. When consumers become producers, they do not have to accept what others present but have the freedom to respond in creative ways. With the interactivity established by network technology, there is a shift from mass production to mass customization. Consider, for example, the way in which the iPod led to a severe weakening in sales of CDs by allowing people to customize their music selection rather than purchase songs they don't want. In one of the most creative uses of the iPhone I know, artist David Hockney is producing and distributing original artwork to individuals on the Web. This model could easily be adapted to create and distribute educational materials. In a later chapter, I will show how these developments reconfigure the responsibilities of teachers and give students more freedom to help fashion their own education.

Fourth, digital technology allows for reproduction without any loss of quality; the copy, in other words, is just as good as the original. Moreover, data can be stored and distributed easily and cheaply. Just as iTunes has transformed the music industry, so Google's digital library, Amazon's Kindle, the iPad and enTourage Systems's eDGe dual-screen multimedia reader are changing publishing in ways that will affect higher education. Indeed, these technologies have already spread to higher education—some colleges and universities are beginning to produce lectures and courses that can be downloaded through iTunes University or iUniversity. On the train, I have overheard students discussing podcasts of lectures they are listening to on their iPods, and once I even saw a person watching the video of a lecture on her iPhone.

Fifth, decentralized interactive networks make it possible for smaller players to have a bigger impact. Exchange no longer takes place merely between an influential center and a marginal periphery, but also among people and organizations across the network. Interactive networks can create disproportionate effects. One of the distinctive characteristics of networks and webs makes this possible. Networks are complex systems that do not follow a one-to-one linear logic. Each node (a node can be an individual user like a student or teacher, an institution, corporation, government agency or even a terror cell) in an interactive web is connected to other nodes and, by extension, to the whole network. Since these networks are interactive, relations are two-way and, thus, nonlinear. In linear systems, the effect of any individual or event is always proportionate to the cause—powerful and influential people have a major impact, and big events create big effects. In nonlinear systems, by contrast, events cycle and recycle through mutually reciprocal loops to create what is known as positive feedback. This process amplifies causal events in ways that generate completely disproportionate effects. Ordinary people can have a major impact and little events can create big effects. Popularizers of scientific and social scientific research have dubbed this phenomenon "the butterfly effect." The most common example they use is a weather system in which a butterfly flapping its wings in the South Pacific triggers a thunderstorm in New York City.

The media and information networks that underlie today's social, political, economic and educational systems work the same way. As information is cycled and recycled, its impact is amplified. In technical jargon that has entered the public lexicon, information spreads virally—the more widely it is distributed, the faster its rate of dissemination. This phenomenon can be most readily observed in Web 2.0, which provides the infrastructure for rapidly proliferating social networks like

MySpace and Facebook, Twitter, YouTube and Flickr. YouTube, for example, generates the same number of hours of footage every six months that it took the combined major cable networks seventy years to produce. Flickr, which like YouTube allows videos to be uploaded, also includes a file of images that increases by four thousand every minute and links one million images to Google Earth every day. The reciprocity of relationships in nonlinear networks creates positive feedback loops that move systems and networks to the tipping point where seemingly minor players and inconsequential events create unexpected disruptions like runaway best sellers, fashion fads, financial bubbles, social upheaval, political revolution and intellectual and cultural trends. As educational institutions become connected in these new networks, the possibility of a realignment of influence and redistribution of financial, intellectual and cultural resources emerges.

Sixth, digital networks make different media fungible (i.e., one kind of data can be exchanged and substituted for another). When information is reduced to bits, different forms of data become interchangeable. More specifically, words, images, video and sound can be created, manipulated and integrated into a single product or work, which can then be transmitted and connected to one or more other works. This synthesis results in layered works that are known as hypertexts, each one studded with hyperlinks enabling immediate access to other relevant texts through the Web. In a digital environment, these texts can include images, video and sound as well as words. Hypertexts can be closed or open. In closed hypertexts, readers, viewers and users are free to navigate through an expansive labyrinth of other works but cannot change the work. In open hypertexts like Wikipedia, users become coauthors who can contribute to the work. In addition to its constantly expanding online encyclopedia, Wikipedia has given away over 210,000 Wikis (i.e., software programs) for K–12 education. This software, which enables people to create works like Wikipedia on any subject for any purpose, has become wildly popular among teachers in primary and secondary schools and is spreading to some colleges and universities. These open hypertexts mimic the structure of the constantly changing and ever-evolving Web through which they circulate.

Finally, the fungibility of data creates the conditions for the use of multifunctional devices, which replace old single-purpose appliances. Whereas in the past it was necessary to have different instruments to process words, images, video and audio, now a single device can deal with information in all of these media. These multipurpose processors continue the trajectory of miniaturization that can be traced from mainframe computers and PCs to cell phones and personal digital assistants (PDAs). The combination of miniaturization and wireless transmission greatly increases mobility and the accessibility of information. In addition, it marks a further stage in the creation of a distributed network that began when PCs replaced mainframe computers. New handheld devices can deliver the data that used to require a large room full of vacuum tubes and wires to handle. The astonishing resolution of images, videos and sounds on these small devices opens many new distribution outlets. Some companies, such as Palm, are already developing educational applications for PDAs. In coming years, these multipurpose devices will be used to deliver both educational materials and actual courses.

Various developments that have been unfolding for the past two decades are coming together to pose new challenges and open new possibilities for higher education. If we are to negotiate the turbulent environment in which we find ourselves, it is essential for people to understand the multiplicity, diversity, interrelation and complexity of the networks shaping our world. The emerging infrastructure of network culture has already transformed manufacturing, transportation, news, media, finance and politics, and it seems likely that its impact on higher education will be no less significant. In many ways, higher education is already entangled in this web. Some faculty members realize the potential of network technologies, others are indifferent and still others see the Internet, the World Wide Web and the multiple media they support as a threat to the very viability of higher education. While every technology has its limitations, it would, in my judgment, be a mistake to overlook the rich possibilities for research, writing, teaching and learning that digital devices and distributed networks create. (We will turn to this discussion shortly.)

These developments do not offer a panacea for higher education, and it remains important to preserve what is valuable in the policies and practices of the past. As I said earlier, it will always be important for students to learn to think critically, read carefully and write well. Moreover, accelerating globalization makes it essential for young people to be exposed to different cultural traditions. I believe the technologies we have been considering will become more rather than less important for society as a whole as well as for higher education. It is, therefore, incumbent upon us to probe their potential for improving education and enriching the lives of everyone. I am suggesting not that we replace the old with the new but that we use the old to help us understand and appreciate the new and use the new to foster innovations, while at the same time supporting those aspects of traditional education that continue to be effective. Financial difficulties, social tensions and political squabbling, however, will make it more and more difficult to muster the material and personal resources necessary to fulfill this mission. It is to that subject that we now turn.

5

Education Bubble

American colleges and universities, businesses that are vital to our national interests, are facing unprecedented financial difficulties. In order to sustain our leadership position in the world, radical changes must be made.

To begin to understand the full scope of the problems, we must evaluate factors that are relevant for any business: assets, costs, liabilities and income. The more one studies the economic plight of colleges and universities, the more disturbing the parallels with the recent failure of banks and other major financial institutions. While many factors within and beyond universities have contributed to this crisis, none has been more important than the transformation of the global financial system brought about by the networking of the world's financial infrastructure. People who believe that the recent financial meltdown is nothing more than another cyclical disruption that eventually will correct itself do not understand what is going on. This crisis is not the result of a few rogue Wall Street bankers or mistaken models and misguided policies; it is systemic. The failure of the global financial system exposes the fragility of the new form of capitalism that has emerged in the past four decades and raises questions about its long-term viability.

On October 19, 1987, Black Monday, the Dow lost 22.6 percent of its value, or $500 billion. That seemed like an inconceivable amount of money at the time. At dinner that night, I had a conversation about the day's events with my son, Aaron, who was fifteen at the time and now works in finance.

"Something really important happened today," I said.

"Yeah, what?"

"In the twinkling of an eye, billions of dollars disappeared into thin air. Just like that!"

"Where'd they go?"

I was taken aback by the question and wasn't sure how to answer.

"Well, I don't exactly know. I guess the money wasn't really there in the first place."

"So, then, what's the big deal?"

Aaron turned out to be right. Within a few months, the market was back to where it was before the crash.

In the years since the 1987 crash, bubble after bubble has burst, and financial assets have become more and more virtual, as opposed to money we can put our hands on at any given time. Who would have thought that our leading universities with what are supposed to be the best economics departments in the world would bet their future on what turned out to be an illusion, hypothetical money? And who could have imagined that some of the most influential advisors to private equity and hedge funds would be distinguished professors at the very institutions whose endowments plummeted as a result of their misguided theories? Supposedly sophisticated economists entranced by thinking about thinking developed algorithms, mathematical tools, to process equations that had little or nothing to do with the real economy but much to do with financial speculation. In previous forms of capitalism, people made money by trading things or selling their own labor; in finance capitalism, by contrast, wealth is generated by trading abstract financial instruments backed by nothing more than virtual assets. It is as if financial engineers created a reverse alchemical process that turned money into worthless paper.

Wall Street bankers and brokers were creating wealth out of thin air with numbers derived from other numbers. During the past two decades, the financial economy has exploded at a rate that defies the imagination. While it is difficult to establish the value of something based on nothing, reliable estimates indicate that in 2007 the total value of the real economy (goods and services) was $47 trillion, and the total value of the financial economy (numbers derived from numbers) was $437 trillion. Alchemy, indeed!

As the bull market, which began in 1982, continued to flourish, individuals and institutions started to borrow money to invest in increasingly speculative derivatives. A derivative is a financial asset whose value derives from some other underlying assets. There are three primary types of derivatives—futures, options and swaps—each of which can involve underlying assets like stocks, bonds, interest rates or currencies. Instead of trading an underlying asset, investors and speculators agree to exchange cash or other assets to hedge against the decline in the value of the underlying asset or to bet on its increase. In this way, derivatives provide a way to shift risk from people who do not want it to people who are willing to bear risk for the possibility of a more profitable return. The growing popularity of these financial products over the past twenty years created secondary and tertiary markets for derivatives. As the derivative drifts farther and farther from markets grounded in underlying assets, its relation to real value becomes more distant and tenuous and markets become much more volatile.

In addition to the explosion of derivative markets, many financial firms, start-ups and traditional businesses became more highly leveraged than ever. A leveraged investment is purchased with borrowed money for which the investor must have a certain percentage of liquid assets (known as collateral) to insure the loan. Throughout the 1990s, regulators allowed a decline in the percentage of required collateral, thereby amplifying the risks attached to loans and increasing the volatility of financial markets. In some cases derivatives were so leveraged that a small change in the value of the underlying asset could cause a big drop in the value of the derivative. As new investment opportunities emerged, investors started borrowing heavily to speculate in financial markets. At the same time, the nature of collateral changed. Instead of securing loans with cash or material assets like factories, equipment and inventory, investors used the very securities they had purchased with the borrowed money as collateral for loans. This practice is dangerously irresponsible because when the price of the security goes down, the value of the collateral declines and the creditor demands more collateral through what is called a margin call. If borrowers have inadequate liquid assets, they have to sell the very stock they used for collateral in order to meet the margin call. This naturally drives the stock price lower and creates a downward spiral in which the decline in stock price leads to a decrease in the value of the collateral, which triggers another margin call that requires the borrower to sell off even more of the stock that is supposed to be securing the loan. This spiral is one of the devastating traps in which university endowments have been caught.

In the 1980s, deregulation even transformed the traditionally cautious savings and loan industry. With most of their assets tied up in long-term loans for home mortgages, which were held at artificially low rates by government regulations, S&Ls were not able to compete with other financial institutions. When the federal government eventually deregulated the interest rates banks could offer investors, rates quickly rose as high as 18 to 20 percent. But this did not solve all of the S&Ls' problems, so the federal government also allowed banks to make real estate investments. Since most bankers had no experience in this area, they made many unwise investments, and many local banks failed.

At the same time that banks were under increasing pressure, the nature of financial markets changed. The introduction of computers on trading floors in the late 1970s and the networking of computers in the 1980s created an opportunity for more complicated derivative products. Thousands of new products for investors were soon introduced. When computers became more sophisticated and networking technology spread, financial instruments became more abstract. As computerized trading programs removed human beings from the trading equation, volatility and risk increased. To any rational investor, it should have been clear that financial markets were becoming a precarious confidence game. But the perpetual hope for a big payoff fueled the madness.

When, in a networked economy, virtual assets disappear into thin air in an instant, as they can on a massive scale, the entire global economy is at risk. As networks expand and more people and institutions are connected, everything speeds up and the stakes grow higher. As we have seen, in complex networks like financial markets, effects can be disproportionate to their causes. In 2008, the collapse of the housing market in the United States quickly set off ripples through world financial networks and triggered a catastrophic collapse of banks and other financial institutions in England, Russia, China, even Iceland. The problem was not simply that individuals had purchased houses that they could not afford but that so-called financial engineers had created derivatives known as mortgage-backed securities and credit default swaps whose risks most investors did not understand. These investments bundled and securitized thousands of individual home mortgages, divided them according to their supposed risk and then sold them on global markets. Mortgage-backed securities were sold and resold to other speculators so many times that they seemed to lose any relation to the actual assets that were supposed to serve as collateral. When the bubble burst, real estate brought virtual assets crashing back to earth.

This financial meltdown has been devastating for college and university endowments and is wreaking havoc with their budgets. The schools had irrational dreams of huge payoffs just like everyone else. The magnitude of the losses and the scale of the problems they engendered will force a rethinking of the entire financial structure of higher education and will require cutbacks and new efficiencies that will bring major organizational changes. Meanwhile, some facts and figures about what has been going on for the past several decades should shed considerable light on the difficulties higher education is facing.

Until recently, colleges and universities followed very conservative investment policies. Many schools managed their endowments in-house with the guidance of a small group of trustees. Through the 1950s, most institutions restricted endowments to cash and fixed-income assets. During the 1960s institutions gradually began to invest some of their endowments in conservative securities. Not until the 1970s and 1980s did they begin to invest significant sums in stocks, and at first they did so cautiously; even the most venturesome portfolios were split into roughly 60 percent securities and 40 percent bonds. Spending policies were also conservative—the widely accepted practice was to spend no more than 5 percent of endowment income and keep everything else as principal as a hedge against inflation. That meant that every dollar spent required twenty to remain in the endowment.

All of this changed dramatically in the 1990s. Many colleges and universities, led by the wealthiest institutions in the country, shifted away from securities and fixed income and moved toward hedge funds and private equity firms, which were profiting from heavy investments in the new financial instruments that had been introduced since the mid-1980s.

Yale's David Swensen led the way. By 2000 he had published *Pioneering Portfolio Management: An Unconventional Approach to Institutional Investment*, which quickly became the bible for advisors charged with investing university endowments. Though he urged caution for less wealthy institutions, he nonetheless concluded, "These findings suggest that long-term investors maximize wealth by investing in high-return, high-risk equity rather than buying debt instruments of governments and corporations." By 2008, Swensen had invested an astonishing 80 percent of Yale's endowment in three unconventional asset groups: hedge funds, private equity funds and so-called real assets like real estate, oil, gas and timber. The requirements imposed by many of these investments rendered a significant percentage of Yale's endowment illiquid.

Though the risks were much higher than universities traditionally had been willing to take, the rewards were impressive, and many other colleges and universities soon started taking notice. Ivy League schools and wealthy universities were the first to adopt Swensen's investment strategy, but then many less wealthy schools got caught up in the frenzy and followed suit. As investments became more complex and markets more volatile, colleges and universities either hired investment specialists or outsourced fund management to private firms.

With this shift toward more volatile assets from the mid-1990s on, colleges and universities saw their returns soar, and endowments grew. In the years prior to the recent financial meltdown, the endowments of leading universities had double-digit returns and rose to record levels. Yale's average annual rate of return was 16.3 percent, and its endowment rose to an unprecedented $22.9 billion. The situation at other elite universities was similar: Harvard, 13.8 percent ($36.9 billion); Stanford, 14.2 percent ($20.4 billion); and Princeton, 14.9 percent ($16.4 billion). Though not all schools were this successful, alternative investments significantly outperformed the S&P 500 for more than a decade.

The financial condition of colleges and universities mirrored the pattern of what was occurring in the broader society at the time. The rich consistently got richer. In 1995 Ivy League endowments were forty times larger than the endowments of public universities, and by 2005 they were seventy times larger. The redistribution of personal wealth created by finance capitalism is important, but so are the implications of the growing divide between the nation's wealthiest institutions and all other colleges and universities. For institutions as well as individuals, power and influence come with money. As greater wealth is concentrated in fewer institutions, the course of higher education is set by a smaller and smaller group of colleges and universities. This restriction of power and influence creates less intellectual diversity, which weakens higher education.

It all came to a sudden end. In *Inside Higher Education,* Jim Wolfston writes:

> On December 16, 2008, president Richard Levin explained to Yale faculty and staff that: "Our best estimate of the Endowment's value today is $17 billion, a decline of 25 percent since June 30, 2008." But what this "best estimate" failed to point out is that in real dollar terms, Yale's sudden six-month loss wiped out the reported endowment return of 22.9 percent for fiscal 2006, the reported 28 percent return for fiscal 2007, *and* the reported return of 4.5 percent for fiscal 2008! By

the Higher Education Price Index, the six-month loss had set the Yale endowment back nearly four years to the same purchasing power it held as of June 30, 2005.

With the unexpected financial collapse in the fall of 2008, a decade of double-digit increases in returns on endowment investments suddenly turned into double-digit losses. For colleges and universities, like banks and financial firms, actual losses are difficult to gauge because it is impossible to determine the actual value of many of the assets. From 2008 to 2009, the value of college and university endowments declined by an average of 23 percent.

Throughout the history of American higher education, Harvard has often charted the course other colleges and universities have followed. This has frequently led to needed reforms, but the consequences of following Harvard's aggressive investment strategy have been devastating for many schools. As I said, at one point, Harvard's endowment reached an unprecedented $36.9 billion; from July to October 2008, this figure reportedly declined by $8 billion. By the spring of 2009, the Faculty of Arts and Sciences, which does not include professional schools, was facing a budget deficit of $220 million. The university had also committed an additional $11 billion to private-equity funds and hedge funds, thereby creating serious liquidity problems. Nina Munk reports in a 2009 *Vanity Fair* article entitled "Rich Harvard, Poor Harvard" that faced with the challenge of immediately cutting the arts and sciences budget by 20 percent, an unnamed administrator conceded, "There are going to be a hell of a lot of layoffs. Courses will be cut. Class sizes will get bigger." Munk proceeds to argue:

> If Harvard were a serious business facing a liquidity crisis, it would have done something drastic by now: fired senior employees, closed departments, sold off real estate. But Harvard, like most other leading universities, is stubborn and inflexible. "None of these schools has the ability to cut expenses fast enough" is how a hedge-fund manager who counts Harvard among his investors explained the problem. Running the numbers for me, proving how impossible it is for a shrinking endowment to keep up with a university's bloated, immovable costs, the hedge-fund manager concluded, "They are completely fucked."

Sometimes facing big problems begins with small steps. In an article published in *The Harvard Crimson* Bonnie Kavoussi and Lauren Kiel report:

> The first Faculty meeting of the year kicked off without a regular staple: cookies to complement professors' tea and coffee.
>
> "This is the first time in modern times with no cookies," Faculty council member Harry R. Lewis

'68 said as he held a white mug of tea. "We're sharing the pain with undergraduates."

"As part of our cost-cutting efforts, we're doing our little part in our Faculty meetings, saving about $500 per meeting for cookies and coffee," Faculty of Arts and Sciences Dean Michael D. Smith explained during the meeting.

With biting irony, students expose the folly of professors who continue to sip tea and avoid hard choices while their world is unraveling around them. If as Harvard goes so goes the country, troubled times lie ahead.

Like the boards of directors of so many banks and investment firms, far too many college and university boards of trustees failed to fulfill their responsibilities for financial oversight. Alumni and donors should demand that the administrators as well as the trustees responsible for those losses be held up to scrutiny, and, if there was financial malfeasance, those involved should be held criminally accountable.

We have discovered that networks become more volatile as they become more complex. With frequent unpredictable disruptions, colleges and universities had little time to act. The situation was exacerbated because most college administrators either didn't understand their liquidity problems or were reluctant to explain them to students, faculty members, alumni and the public. Hedge and private equity funds require investors to commit money for a set period of time, and do not allow withdrawal without costly penalties. Thus, educational institutions with these investments could not sell their plummeting assets to free up income needed to cover other losses and ongoing operating expenses. They had no backup plan. Out of avarice, most schools had let cash reserves slip below 5 percent. In June 2009, *Barron's* reported that faced with little liquidity and declining revenues, several Ivy League universities were forced to take drastic measures. "To give themselves financial breathing room and forestall asset sales, major universities sold sizable amounts of debt last year. Harvard issued $1.5 billion; Princeton, $1 billion; and Yale, $800 million. Harvard's debt now exceeds $5 billion. Even while borrowing heavily, many big universities have been sellers of stocks, bonds and other liquid assets in the past year." Less wealthy schools have not been able to sell their way out of immediate financial distress so easily. Though financial managers deny it, there is a strong likelihood that increasing universities' debt burden will compound the problems in the near future. There is a real possibility that some colleges and universities, like major banks, will not be able to meet their day-to-day obligations and will fail.

To compound the problem, many educational institutions have been living beyond their means for almost two decades. Colleges and universities, like the rest of the country, went on a spending spree and debt mounted. As endowments rose, schools became more ambitious, and competition for students increased. To make themselves more attractive to students and improve their place in the *U.S. News & World Report* rankings, administrators engaged in a construction race. In some cases, new construction was for legitimate academic purposes; most of it was not. To attract students, especially those who do not need financial aid, colleges and universities built expensive athletic facilities and student centers as well as five-star dorms with big entertainment and recreational amenities. They borrowed heavily on credit markets that had become less and less stable to finance these projects. In the past, most responsible institutions did not begin the construction of a building until they had raised the money for it as well as funds for an endowment to cover future maintenance. But following the lead of the banks from whom they borrowed millions, ambitious administrators borrowed money with little or no collateral, thereby leveraging their institutions. To make matters worse, they borrowed most of this money at variable interest rates and so could not be sure about the extent of their exposure. When rates went up, colleges and universities had to either pay more or draw on already depleted endowments to pay back the principal.

A. Richard Kneedler, a consultant on higher education and former president of Franklin & Marshall College, underscores the magnitude of the problem when he concludes that an astonishing two thirds of the seven hundred private colleges he examined are at risk of financial failure. By the spring of 2009, the financial condition of 114 private colleges was so fragile that they failed to meet the financial-responsibility guidelines that the Department of Education uses to measure the health of colleges and universities.

As of July 2009, Harvard's debt had risen to $6 billion. Munk reports, "Servicing this debt alone will cost Harvard an average of $517 million *a year* through 2038, according to Standard and Poor's." That is a figure considerably greater than the total endowment of most colleges. Other elite institutions are in a similar bind. Since 1987, Middlebury College's debt has ballooned from a manageable $5 million to an onerous $270 million. On May 29, 2009, *The Wall Street Journal* carried an article reporting that Dartmouth College was stripped of its triple-A rating as a result of investment losses in the endowment. Moody's Investors Service had already downgraded twenty other universities and recorded a negative outlook for the credit rating of fifty-five additional schools. During the first half of 2009, twelve schools with double-A or triple-A ratings collectively borrowed $6 billion to meet financial obligations and operating expenses. Such short-term tactics are bound to lead to more difficulties because they violate a simple maxim: you cannot borrow your way out of debt.

At the same time that the value of assets (i.e., endowments) is going down and liabilities (i.e., debts) are going up, costs for colleges and universities continue to rise. Most of these costs are fixed and leave very little room to maneuver. The increase in the cost of maintaining the physical plant and providing food and housing for students, faculty and administrators shows no signs of slowing down. The size of administrations and staffs has grown at a significantly higher rate than the size of faculties for more than a decade. In some cases, these new positions were created to meet perceived demands from consumers; in others, they are unjustified and increase an already top-heavy bureaucracy. During the same period that the number of employees has been growing, their pay and salaries have been increasing faster than the rate of inflation.

While costs continue to rise, income is not improving. There are four basic sources of income for colleges and universities: private donations; local, state and government support; tuition; and partnerships and collaborations with private corporations and businesses. Revenues from all but the last are declining and are unlikely to recover in the foreseeable future. Donations always go up and down with the overall economy and the movement of financial markets. Though it is too early to know what lasting impact current economic problems will have on charitable giving, donations and bequests are declining and will probably take a long time to recover. According to a recent report in *The Chronicle of Higher Education,* 60 percent of institutions reported a decline in giving in 2009. The median decrease was 45.7 percent. The situation in the public sector is no better than in the private. With declining tax revenues and increasing demands on budgets, the support of local, state and federal governments for education is decreasing at every level. In the 1960s and 1970s, it was assumed that the public should pay for 70 to 80 percent of the cost of higher education; today many public universities receive less than 10 percent of their operating budgets from the government. If this continues, the line separating public and private institutions, which is already obscure, will disappear altogether. The privatization of all higher education would leave colleges and universities free to raise prices even higher.

These developments further increase the financial pressure on students and their families. Income has to come from somewhere. During the past twenty-five years, tuition and fees have gone up 440 percent, which is four times the rate of inflation.

According to a 2009 Congressional report, since 1981, the average cost of four years of college has increased 202 percent, while the consumer price index has gone up only 80 percent.

Numbers and graphs remain abstract until they are applied to individual cases. Consider what the increase

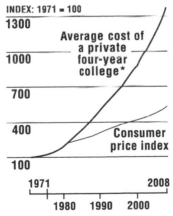

INDEX: 1971 = 100

Average cost of a private four-year college*

Consumer price index

*Four-year private degree-granting institutions

Increase in Cost of College, 1971–2008

Fortune, April 27, 2009

in the cost of college will mean for students and their parents in the next two decades. Using figures from the College Board, The SmartStudent Guide to Financial Aid concludes, "It would be reasonable to expect an average inflation rate of 7 percent or 8 percent for the next ten years." The implications of this prediction are staggering. The chart on page 103 shows the price of a four-year college education at a top-tier school for the next two decades. I have based these calculations on a current cost of $50,000 and have the more conservative estimate of a 6 percent annual increase. It is hard to comprehend these figures. In 2020 four years at a private college will cost $328,890, a decade later the price will have increased to $588,992 and by 2035 the sticker price will be $788,205. Obviously, this situation is unsustainable.

Financial aid and government support will not be able to keep pace with inflation. Pell Grants already cover less than half of what they covered for a year at a state college or university three decades ago. During the recent economic boom, many colleges and universities increased student aid. A few elite schools remain committed to aid-blind admissions policies, and Harvard and Princeton went so far as to institute a zero family contribution for applicants from families with incomes below $60,000. These laudable programs, which have been financed by healthy endowments, are now in jeopardy. Williams recently announced that it is reinstituting student loans rather than providing scholarships to cover all financial aid. With dwindling resources and increasing demand for financial aid, fewer students who

Education Bubble

Academic Year	One-Year Cost	Four-Year Cost	Class Entering	Class Graduating
2009–10	50,000			
2010–11	53,000			
2011–12	56,180			
2012–13	59,551	218,731	2009	2013
2013–14	63,124	231,855	2010	2014
2014–15	66,911	245,766	2011	2015
2015–16	70,926	260,512	2012	2016
2016–17	75,182	276,143	2013	2017
2017–18	79,692	292,711	2014	2018
2018–19	84,474	310,274	2015	2019
2019–20	89,542	328,890	2016	2020
2020–21	94,915	348,624	2017	2021
2021–22	100,610	369,541	2018	2022
2022–23	106,646	391,714	2019	2023
2023–24	113,045	415,216	2020	2024
2024–25	119,828	440,129	2021	2025
2025–26	127,018	466,537	2022	2026
2026–27	134,639	494,529	2023	2027
2027–28	142,717	524,201	2024	2028
2028–29	151,280	555,653	2025	2029
2029–30	160,357	588,992	2026	2030
2030–31	169,978	624,332	2027	2031
2031–32	180,177	661,792	2028	2032
2032–33	190,987	701,499	2029	2033
2033–34	202,447	743,589	2030	2034
2034–35	214,594	788,205	2031	2035

Projected Cost in Dollars for Four Years at a
Private College, 2010–2035
(Calculated Annual Increase of 6 Percent)

need assistance are going to be admitted. In the spring of 2009 prestigious Reed College dropped more than one hundred needy students who had been judged worthy of acceptance and substituted less-qualified students who could pay what is commonly described as the sticker price. It is not clear how much longer even the wealthiest colleges and universities will be able to afford aid-blind admissions.

Though there is growing recognition of the problem, there is no consensus about how to deal with it. One proposal circulated in Washington called for securitizing student loans and selling the debt on financial markets. That is, we should solve the financial problems of higher education by turning them over to the bankers who brought us securitized mortgages and credit default swaps!

In the short term, college and university enrollments continue to rise. Indeed, when economic times are tough, everyone seeks a competitive edge, and college looks attractive. There is, however, no guarantee that enrollment growth will continue. Nationwide only half the students who begin college receive a four-year degree. With rising costs and less money available for financial aid, more and more students will be forced to trade down by attending cheaper schools, and a growing number of young people will be unable to afford to attend any school. A decline in enrollments would be devastating for financially strapped schools that depend on tuition income.

Faced with pressure from every side, the tried-and-true sales pitch of colleges and universities no longer rings quite so true. For years, admissions officers have been hawking their product by claiming that over their careers, college graduates on average earn more than twice as much as non–college graduates. But with a price tag of $220,000 for four years at an elite college or university and an average of $122,000 for all private schools, and rising, and with only 19 percent of the class of 2009 with jobs at the time they graduated, many students and their parents are beginning to ask whether it is worth going deeper and deeper into debt for four years of study that often does not prepare graduates for contemporary life and thus holds little promise of employment. In a 2009 article in *The New York Times* entitled "The College Calculation: How Much Does Higher Education Matter?" David Leonhardt asks a question that is heard with increasing frequency: "How much does a college education—the actual teaching and learning that happens on campus—really matter?" The findings he reports should raise concern for people involved in higher education.

Last month, National Public Radio ran a segment called "Is a College Education Worth the Debt?" in which an economist noted that 12 percent of mail carriers have college degrees—the point being that they could have gotten the same jobs without the degrees. In January [2009], "20/20" ran a similar segment, in which somebody identified as an education consultant and a career counselor summed up the case against college. "You could take the pool of collegebound students and you could lock them in a closet for four years," he said, and thanks to their smarts and work ethic, they would still outearn people who never went to college. I heard a more measured version of these concerns when I recently sat down with a group of college students. They were paying tuition and studying hard, and yet they weren't sure what they would find on the other side of graduation.

In the past several years, I have also heard similar concerns voiced by many of my students. While the value of a college education is surely more than financial, it would be a mistake not to take the growing apprehension about the cost-effectiveness of higher education seriously.

Plummeting assets, increasing liabilities, decreasing liquidity, increasing costs, debt crises for governments, colleges, universities, students and parents, and on top of all of this decreasing revenue—this is not exactly a prescription for financial health.

With these thoughts swirling through my head, I left my office on a beautiful day last spring to attend the final meeting of department chairs for the year. Workers in the Columbia quad were busy assembling the platforms and bleachers where forty thousand students, family, friends and faculty would soon gather to celebrate commencement. Kids were tossing Frisbees and lounging on the library steps. The beautiful wood-paneled room in which we met was sealed off from the buzz and excitement of the surrounding campus and city. The meeting began, as many others had recently, with a report on the university's financial condition. While exact figures would not be available until September, it was already clear that the endowment would be down at least 30 percent. Sober administrators summarized what steps had already been taken: a 5 percent cut in the current operating budget, a university-wide hiring freeze, a freeze on all salaries and wages, a 10 percent cut in graduate student admissions and a 10 percent increase in undergraduate student admissions. Not much more could be done, they said, without cutting into bone. Layoffs at this point did not seem likely, but they were already occurring at other universities, and nothing could be ruled out. Faculty and staff, however, would decline through attrition. The vice president then methodically walked faculty members through the details of the budget for the current fiscal year and the tentative projections for the next two budget cycles. Since the university was heavily invested in hedge funds and private-equity funds, he had to admit uncertainty about the projections in the face of continuing budgetary pressures. In the best-case scenario, expendable income from the endowment for the arts and sciences budget would decrease at an annual rate of "only" 8 percent for the next three years. When a faculty member asked how long it would be until budgets returned to precrash levels, the provost answered, "Not for the foreseeable future."

Our nation's public universities are facing even more severe financial problems. Declining tax revenues and increasing expenses have led to significant cutbacks in state funding across the country. On the day I am writing these words (October 3, 2009), Bob Herbert published an op-ed article entitled "Cracks in the Future" in *The New York Times*. Herbert wrote:

> While the U.S. has struggled with enormous problems over the past several years, there has been at least one consistent bright spot. Its system of higher education has remained the finest in the world.
>
> Now there are ominous cracks appearing in that cornerstone of American civilization. Exhibit A is the University of California, Berkeley, the finest public university in the world and undoubtedly one of the two or three best universities in the United States, public or private. . . .
>
> It's dismaying to realize that the grandeur of Berkeley (and the remarkable success of the University of California system, of which Berkeley is the flagship) is being jeopardized by shortsighted politicians and California's colossally dysfunctional budget processes.

The California system, which has taken decades to develop and has provided important opportunities for countless students and faculty members, is unraveling with astonishing rapidity. In late 2009, Robert Birgeneau, chancellor of UC Berkeley, reported that his university had to cut $150 million in fiscal year 2009–2010 and $814 million from the state's higher education as a whole. The latest cuts come on top of significant reductions over the past two decades. State support, corrected for inflation and enrollment, is down almost two thirds since 1991–1994. In an article entitled "In California, a Teachable Crisis," published in *The Chronicle of Higher Education* in the fall of 2009, Christopher Newfield describes a budgetary process that defies reason. After cutting $814 million, the governor's Department of Finance "threw all of the university's federal stimulus money into the hole that created—resulting in a net loss of 5 percent. Then it cut an additional $637 million for 2009–10, leaving the university's state general-fund budget down 25 percent for 2008–10." Neither short-term nor long-term planning is possible in the midst of such chaos. To make up for these budget cuts, administrators predict that it will be necessary to raise tuition from $8,000 to $15,000. By some estimates, the annual cost for attending a university in the California system would have to increase as much as $30,000 to get back to the 2001 level of support. To appreciate just how desperate this situation has become, it is helpful to note that in the early 1960s tuition for the entire year was approximately $150.

The measures already taken include faculty and staff cutbacks, a hiring freeze, a major decrease in faculty support (telephones were recently removed from all faculty offices), significant curtailments of student services and a reduction in the money available for financial aid. Faculty and staff had even been asked to take unpaid furloughs of between twenty-one and twenty-six days (the lower the salary the fewer the days) a year. University officials fear that even these draconian measures might not be sufficient. With falling tax revenues caused by a sluggish economy, the university is bracing for cuts that could be even worse next year. While these problems are to a significant degree the result of an outdated and regressive tax system combined with endless legislative gridlock, the crisis unfolding in California is nonetheless a sign of the unprecedented challenges all public and private colleges and universities are facing. Herbert concluded, "The problems at Berkeley are particularly acute because of the state's drastic reduction of support. But colleges and universities across the country—public and private—are struggling because of the prolonged economic crisis and the pressure on state budgets. It will say a great deal about what kind of nation we've become if we let these most valuable assets slip into a period of decline."

Honesty compels us to admit that the financial resources necessary to meet the needs of higher education are not likely to be forthcoming for the foreseeable future. If the current economic downturn is not cyclical but rather a symptom of deeper long-term changes, these difficulties will not only persist but worsen. Even if ample funding were available, it would not solve all of our problems.

Developments in higher education since the 1960s have created internal divisions and tensions in colleges and especially research universities that are deepening as financial resources become more scarce. It is possible that this moment of crisis will provide an opportunity to rethink not only how to fund higher education but also what goes on in college and university libraries, laboratories and classrooms. Meeting these challenges must begin with a frank acknowledgment of the magnitude of the problem and will require a level of cooperation that is, unfortunately, rare on most college and university campuses. Faculty members, administrators, staff and students must work together to find creative solutions that will create a vital and viable system of higher education for the future. I will be making suggestions to foster these goals in the chapters that follow.

6

Networking Knowledge

As we have seen, the university and the wider world have been moving in opposite directions for the past half century. Emerging technologies have accelerated the process of globalization in ways that increase interconnections among people, countries and institutions. New forms of transportation and communication are bringing more people across the world into greater contact than ever before. As people become more closely connected, their differences often become more obvious and misunderstandings lead to conflict. With these developments, the urgency of learning other languages and studying other cultures in all of their diversity and complexity becomes vital. In addition, new media and communications technologies have triggered explosive growth in the amount of information to which people have ready access. Not only is the quantity of information growing, its substance is also changing. This has important implications for the reorganization of knowledge and, by extension, higher education. As cross-cultural communication grows, it transforms old assumptions and ideas. Higher education must find new ways to adapt to these changes.

While the world has been moving toward greater interconnection and interdependence, universities have become increasingly fragmented internally. There are many reasons why. In the arts and humanities, political correctness and identity politics have created deep fissures and serious tensions, which have been exacerbated by the growing diversity of both faculties and student bodies. No less important, however, has been the mounting pressure for faculty members to produce and publish original research. The pressure is, of course, greatest at research universities, but it has, for reasons I will consider in a later chapter, trickled down to all universities and colleges. As the demands for publication have increased, areas of research have become more and more specialized. This has led to the identification of specialization with expertise. What often gets overlooked in today's intellectual climate is that expertise does not always have to be defined in terms of a specific subfield but also can be cultivated by examining the ways in which fields usually kept apart are also interrelated. For example, expertise in economics that is limited to mathematics is inadequate and needs to be supplemented with expertise in the relationship between economics and psychology, sociology and even religion.

The narrowing of research focus leads to a restriction of interest that makes communication among different departments and disciplines more and more difficult. The situation in the modern university is reminiscent of the late eighteenth-century German poet Friedrich Schiller's description of modern humanity's alienation. "Everlastingly chained to a single little fragment of the whole, modern man himself develops into nothing but a fragment; everlastingly in his ear the monotonous sound of the wheel that he turns, he never develops the harmony of his being, and instead of putting the stamp of humanity upon his own nature, becomes nothing more than the imprint of his occupation or his specialized knowledge." The problem has become far worse than the gulf between the sciences and the humanities that C. P. Snow described in his influential 1959 book *The Two Cultures*. Not only do humanists and scientists speak different languages, but many humanists are actually unable or unwilling to communicate with one another. Territorial disputes and methodological arguments divide faculties in ways that often make cooperation and collaboration all but impossible. As competition for limited resources increases, these tensions are likely to deepen.

Because the basic structure of the university still conforms to the blueprint Kant drew in 1798, there remains a division between professional schools, which prepare people for specific careers (law, medicine, nursing, journalism, architecture, social work, teaching, public health and engineering), and the faculty of arts and sciences. Most faculties of arts and sciences are organized in three divisions (natural sciences, social sciences and arts and humanities), which sometimes are divided even further. All individual departments are distributed among these three divisions. The division in which a department is located shapes the approach to the subject matter. In some schools, for example, the study of religion is included in the social sciences, and in other schools it is in the arts and humanities. The work done by people in these respective departments is substantially different. When religion is in the division of arts and humanities, literary, philosophical and theological approaches are more common, and when it is in the division of social sciences, psychological, sociological and anthropological approaches, which often are highly empirical and quantitative, are much more common. While many colleges and universities have developed interdepartmental programs, the real locus of power and influence is still the individual department. There has been virtually no effort to rethink the basic departmental structure or to explore other alternatives that might be better suited to today's interconnected world.

The narrow research of faculty members and rigid departmental organization have a negative effect on teaching and students. As the value of research and publication has gone up, the value of teaching has gone down. I will consider this issue in more detail below. For the moment, it is sufficient to note that, while there are many fine teachers devoted to the needs of their students, too many courses represent what the professor wants to teach rather than what students need to learn. Since there is every reason for faculty members to coordinate their research and teaching, many courses for undergraduates as well as graduates have quite narrow parameters. These problems are compounded by the dearth of courses designed to integrate different aspects of students' education.

I first became concerned about the ways in which specialization was making communication among faculty colleagues more difficult during my stay at the National Humanities Center in 1982. The Center supports scholars working in different areas of the humanities for up to one year. I was struck during my stay by how little participants talked to one another about their work and how much trouble they had communicating on the few occasions when they tried to do so. Fellows rarely ventured beyond their private offices for anything other than social reasons. When I returned to Williams, sensitive to the issue, I noticed the same problem on campus. I therefore proposed a Center for the Humanities and Social Sciences, designed to break down departmental and disciplinary boundaries. Through fellowships for faculty members and undergraduate students, interdisciplinary faculty seminars and wide-ranging public lectures and conferences, the center quickly became the focus for lively intellectual discussion on campus and is still thriving. My experience in designing, creating and directing the Williams Center encouraged me to explore other ways to forge channels of communication among faculty members that would break down barriers separating disciplines and dividing departments.

By the late 1980s, I detected another important

problem—with the rapid spread of personal computers, there was a growing gulf between faculty members and students, which seemed to be more than the traditional generation gap. I knew that if I were going to be an effective teacher moving forward, I would have to learn how to bridge that gulf. I started by becoming a student of my students.

The day I realized the world was shifting beneath my feet was November 14, 1992. I was teaching an experimental course at Williams entitled Imagologies: Media Philosophy, with my colleague Esa Saarinen, from the University of Helsinki. Using what was then the latest teleconferencing technology, ten students in Williamstown, Massachusetts, where Williams is located, and ten students in Helsinki met weekly for two hours to discuss the philosophical implications of new media, information and communications technology. Our plan was to create a global classroom in which anybody anywhere in the world could sit around a table and talk together about important issues. It was the first time anything like that had been done, and our experiment attracted considerable media attention. At the time the course began, none of the students had ever used e-mail, but within a few weeks everyone was online regularly. Much to my surprise, a genuine educational community unlike anything I had ever experienced began to emerge.

I did not, however, fully grasp what was transpiring until I was talking with students one afternoon in the computer lab. Cynthia Llamas, a young woman in the class, was intently staring at the screen, completely oblivious to what was going on around her.

"What are you doing?" I asked.

"Playing a MUD," she replied.

"What's that?"

"It's a Multi-User Dungeon."

"Dungeon?"

"Yeah, like Dungeons and Dragons except it's a real-time virtual world. It's interactive and has an online chat room for everybody who is playing."

"Chat room?"

"Well, it's sorta like those old party-line phones my grandmother used to tell me about."

"Where is it?"

"The server is at the University of Texas."

"No, not the server, the game. Where are the other players?"

Staring at me with a puzzled look on her face, Cynthia pointed to the screen in front of her and replied, "They're in there, of course." That was the Aha! moment in which I knew the world had changed and that my students and I were living in different zones. For Cynthia and the other students, everyone was present together in the space-time of the network.

The discussions in our global classroom were unexpectedly lively, and all the students actively participated. Indeed, students were more willing to contribute than in most of my traditional courses. The range of perspectives students brought to the class greatly enriched our discussions. I especially remember the class in which we discussed the French philosopher Jean Baudrillard's book *America*. The Finnish and American students interpreted the book in completely different ways. When the Finnish students readily accepted Baudrillard's rather predictably French criticism of the United States as a country uninterested in history and preoccupied with popular culture, the Williams students pushed back. At one point, Brian Malone, an unusually bright student who now is a professor of neuroscience, declared, "Look, what you Finns don't understand is that for us, Europe is Grandma's attic." This exchange provided an unusual teachable moment.

Obviously, teleconferencing cannot replicate the advantages of the personal when everyone is present in the same room, but my Finnish colleague and I were both surprised by how effectively it simulated what goes on in real classrooms. In moments of intense debate, I sometimes forgot I was on the opposite side of the Atlantic Ocean from Esa and his students. Without this technology, it would not have been possible for students from Finland and the United States to take a class together. By the end of the semester, several of the students had developed close personal relationships through their online discussion. On the last day of class, the Finnish students shocked us when they announced that they and Esa were all coming to Williamstown at their own expense for a week in January.

With the end of the semester drawing near, Esa and I explained the term paper assignment, and the students rebelled. "After what we've been reading and discussing, it makes no sense to write a traditional term paper with footnotes and all that stuff. Let us make a film or video; better yet, how about multimedia projects?" We knew they had a point, but we did not have the resources or ability to support such new forms of creative expression. We admitted they were right, explained our handicap and promised somehow to accommodate what they were proposing the next time around.

The only way I could fulfill my promise to those students, to enter their world, was to develop a collaborative relationship with them. I would teach them the books and ideas I thought were important, and they would teach me about the technologies that were such a significant part of their lives. Students were required to explore the implications of the writings of philosophers and theorists like Søren Kierkegaard, Karl Marx, Martin Heidegger, Jacques Derrida, Maurice Merleau-Ponty, Ernst Gombrich and Marshall McLuhan for the new technologies we were using in class. Our goal was to bring together theory and practice in a way that would enable students to think critically about the media they were using and to consider carefully the social, political, economic and ethical questions new technologies raise. This pedagogical principle continues to inform all of my work with new media. My experience in that first course forced me to admit that if I could not find ways to communicate with students in the media to which they were becoming accustomed, I could never teach them the lessons I thought they should learn. Over the intervening years, I have worked with students to create laboratories in which they learn how to develop arguments, express ideas and communicate with others using a wide range of new media. (I will describe these labs shortly.) Along the way, my own thinking, research, writing and teaching have been transformed.

As I look back, it is hard to believe that less than twenty years ago students at elite American colleges and leading European universities had never used e-mail. With the speed of technological change accelerating, the gap between the teachers and students has increased. Having never known a world without the Internet, today's students take media and communications technologies so much for granted that they do not realize how their new goggles transform their view of the world. Many older faculty members resist learning about and using these technologies. Younger faculty members are more familiar with this new world, but many who would like to develop more experimental styles of teaching and publishing have told me that senior colleagues discourage them from doing so because they say it will take time away from writing scholarly articles and monographs and thus will hurt their chances for tenure. To me, this is folly. The challenge, rather, is to build on the strengths of traditional methods while at the same time exploiting the possibilities of new technologies.

My experience in the Helsinki seminar and the interest it generated led to two additional ventures that suggest intriguing possibilities that might be further explored. As I tried to fulfill my commitment to become a student of my students, I learned about many new possibilities for research and teaching. In the early 1990s, the World Wide Web had not yet been developed. There was, however, inexpensive software for creating multimedia works (i.e., works incorporating written text, images, video and sound), which was readily available and easy to use. Students taught me how to use this software. When the Web appeared and more graphic capabilities and browsers were introduced, we began creating work for the Web. Some interested colleagues asked how they could learn to use these technologies. One of the problems faculty members in the arts and humanities face is that there are almost no public or private agencies that offer grants to purchase the equipment needed to use new media. To address this need and meet these interests, I established a Center for Technology in the Arts and the Humanities at Williams. With the help of the college's Office of Information Technology, we created a laboratory with state-of-the-art equipment for working in digital media. Following the lesson I had learned from my teaching, faculty were paired with students who taught them how to use the hardware and software and introduced them to the kinds of things they could do with these new media. As they experimented, faculty members began integrating the results of their work in their classes. One of the most successful projects developed in the media lab was a series of virtual renderings of medieval cathedrals done by a professor of art and architecture.

A second exciting development came out of the Helsinki seminar. At the suggestion of a student who had been in the seminar, I started distributing my courses at Williams on the Web in 1995. We began by transmitting online an audio and video version of my course on the psychology of religion. People in distant locations could take the class in real time or view it later. The first time I offered this course online over six hundred alumni took it. I then proposed that Williams start a cybercollege for alums, which would distribute at least two online courses every semester. The college was not interested, but an alumnus, Herbert Allen, who is a leading New York investment banker, thought the idea was worth pursuing and offered to back it financially. A few months later, in 1999, we founded Global Education Network (GEN), whose mission was to make high-quality online courses in the liberal arts, humanities and sciences available at a reasonable price to people of all ages anywhere in the world. Our plan was to enter into a collaborative relationship with universities, colleges and professors to produce and distribute courses and other educational materials over the Internet. While there was much interest in the venture, we ultimately failed because of the resistance of faculty members who did not think this way of teaching would be effective and refused to consider any involvement with a for-profit venture, even if their own institutions were equity partners. Though we failed, we learned many important lessons.

When we started the company, our courses consisted

largely of recorded lectures by outstanding university and college professors. We quickly discovered, however, that the talking-heads format hardly took advantage of what the Web had to offer. We changed our strategy, creating courses that included some lecture material but consisted primarily of a rich array of media, ranging from print and film to tape recordings and music. While many of our courses were successful, the most effective one we developed was for the State University of New York system. Working with four of their best professors, we created a course in American history that students throughout the system could use to fulfill one of their graduation requirements. Each course included a required online discussion section, and all courses had papers, quizzes and exams.

Through my work with GEN, I came to understand that digital and networking technologies create different possibilities for organizing knowledge and structuring courses. As we attempted to market our classes, we discovered that some people did not want to take the whole semester and that others wanted to combine elements of courses. In response to this demand, we broke some of our offerings into small units ranging from a single class to a week or an entire semester. People could take any part of a course that interested them, or that they felt they needed. We called this practice "unbundling" courses.

As our thinking developed and our strategy changed, those of us involved in the venture came to understand what we were producing differently. As a lifelong teacher, I envisioned GEN as an extension of the class-room. My goal in the Helsinki seminar was to create a place where anyone from anywhere could come together around the seminar table. Jon Newcomb, who was then the CEO of Simon & Schuster and a member of GEN's board of directors, understood our courses to be an extension of textbooks. With new interactive multimedia, the book has been significantly transformed, and for Jon, online courses were the next logical step after textbooks with CD-ROMs. In fact, the courses we developed were something like a hybrid between a class and a book.

By altering the way information is distributed and knowledge is shared, telecommunications technologies obscure the long-standing line between publication and teaching. At the same time that more and more books and journals are being published electronically, class-rooms are being wired for videoconferencing as well as real-time and delayed audio transmission. With easy-to-use software and hardware, lectures and seminars can be readily transmitted across the globe. The increasing quality of reception on digital devices like mobile phones, the Kindle, iPod and eDGe further extends the range and availability of courses offered on the Web. With these developments, webcasts and podcasts make publication in the form of online teaching virtually ubiquitous and thus available to everyone. As networks spread and the demand for content grows, there will be new opportunities for creating and distributing educational materials.

These innovations are beginning to have a significant impact not only on the method of delivery but on the structure and content of courses. There are currently three kinds of courses: traditional (in-school) courses, online courses in virtual classrooms and courses that combine the former and the latter. As colleges and universities grapple with financial pressures and the cost of higher education continues to escalate, it is going to be increasingly difficult for many schools and students to continue offering courses solely as they have in the past. To meet growing demand with fewer resources, virtual courses will become more popular. It is therefore important for educators to work to make this new way of teaching as effective as possible.

If our experience with GEN is any guide, it seems likely that the structure of courses will become more flexible and less standardized. The format and delivery method of courses in most colleges and universities have changed relatively little over the years. Courses come in three sizes—large (lecture), medium (discussion) and small (seminar)—and all are of roughly the same duration, running for twelve to sixteen weeks in sessions of one to three hours at a time. Most courses are sequentially numbered and ordered hierarchically according to the degree of specialization and level of difficulty. College-wide faculty committees routinely review courses, but the control of the structure and content lies in the hands of the professor.

This standardized format works well and is even necessary for some courses. For example, one must learn basic mathematics before studying physics and must master fundamental chemical processes before proceeding to study organic chemistry and molecular biology. But there is no reason this needs to be the sole organizational principle. It is also possible to create courses that are composed of interrelated sections ordered and combined in different ways. For example, at GEN we produced three survey courses on modernism: modern philosophy, modern music and modern art. In contrast to the standardized format, people could take the whole course or, customizing, select parts of different courses and combine them in different ways. One person chose to combine sections on Hegel, Beethoven and Kandinsky to form her own distinctive course, which proved to be very effective. As the networking of knowledge grows, these webs will not be limited in time and space. Past courses will be stored online, and courses currently being offered at other institutions throughout the world will be available in real time or stored for use at a later time. For example, a class on Melville and a course on his Civil War poetry might be linked with another English class on British war poetry of the twentieth century and a history class on the Civil War. Or a class on James Turrell's art could be linked to courses on Quakerism, perceptual psychology and Hopi spiritual practices, all of which influence his work profoundly. Finally, a course on twentieth-century Protestant fundamentalism could draw on a course about the use of media in religion as well as courses on the religious background of contemporary neoconservative politics and the philosophical foundations of neoliberal economics.

As these courses evolve, they begin to assume the structure of hypertexts. Courses, in other words, are composed by connecting and layering other courses or parts of courses. In this way the individual course is embedded in the constantly expanding and changing web of courses that constitutes the curriculum. Moreover, the curricula of different colleges and universities can also be linked to one another. To glimpse the possibilities this network of courses creates, imagine a catalog of readily available courses as rich and diverse as Google's global library and then think how they could be combined and recombined to create different courses. This is what a truly global education network would look like. Such a design would enable students, with the guidance of professors and academic counselors, to appropriate materials from different sources and create multiple pathways through the courses they are taking. This could be done for hybrid courses that combine real and virtual components as well as for courses that are completely online. As delivery and distribution systems change, courses are no longer restricted to the broadcast model of one-to-many communication, but can become many-to-many conversations that allow for more interactivity than courses that are delivered in university halls where hundreds of students gather to watch a "real" professor on large video screens.

This more flexible course structure can also help alleviate financial pressure on students and their families. When this method of course design and distribution system becomes widespread, students no longer will have to take an entire course, but will be able to take or, in more precise terms, to purchase, any portion of a course—a single session, a few weeks, the entire semester. In education, as in other networked media, mass production is going to give way to mass customization in which students will have considerably more freedom of choice and power. But they will still need guidance. For this system to work effectively, the role of faculty members will change—they not only will teach but increasingly will serve as academic counselors, who advise students on designing courses and selecting programs offered at different institutions. In this arrangement, the professor-student relationship becomes considerably more collaborative. In the courses on media and technology that I have designed with undergraduates, I have found that such collaboration works effectively and is almost always mutually productive.

This reconfiguration of courses not only gives students more freedom but also creates the possibility of decreasing the time necessary to complete a degree, thereby lowering the cost of a college education. Students already can reduce that time by taking advanced placement classes as well as extra courses. But these measures are inadequate given the skyrocketing cost of college. Just as it is not reasonable for every course to be the same length, so it is not necessary to make every student spend four years in college to receive a degree. Rather than requiring all students to complete the same number of courses or to accumulate a certain number of credits, colleges and universities should require students to demonstrate the mastery of knowledge about a particular subject or in a certain area. The means by which the mastery of knowledge is demonstrated can be adjusted for different levels and in different fields. Instead of considering each course a separate unit that is assessed independently, evaluation could take a broader approach that would encourage the integration of a student's course of study. As we will see in the next chapter, students should not only be required to develop competence on a specific subject but should also have to complete an interdisciplinary program focused on a particular problem or theme that complements his or her concentrated work. A student's progress can be measured by conventional oral and written exams and papers as well as exercises in other media that are evaluated by faculty members in each of these areas. It would also be useful to have a culminating assessment that would require students to bring together the different areas, subjects and problems they have studied. While these exercises would be less frequent than traditional course papers and exams, they would be significantly longer and more substantial. The principle of evaluation should always be the same: the *quality* of knowledge rather than the *quantity* of courses is the measure of accomplishment.

To illustrate how a more open and flexible structure of knowledge might be created and what the shift from a closed grid to an open network might look like in practice, I will describe an undergraduate course entitled Real Fakes that I have taught at Williams. One of my aims in this course was to weaken traditional departmental divisions and disciplinary boundaries by bringing together writers, artists, subjects, texts and media that are usually held apart and studied separately. Real Fakes explored the age-old question of the relationship between the original and the copy in different historical eras and various media. Here is the catalog description:

> Cloning, genetic engineering, transplants, implants, cosmetic surgery, artificial life, artificial intelligence, nanotechnology, faux fashion, sampling, plagiarism, art forgery, art about art, photographs of photographs, films about films, identity theft, facial transplants, derivatives, mortgage-backed securities, swaps, Enron, virtual reality, reality TV, Viagra, fake Viagra. The line that has long separated fake/real, artificial/natural, illusory/true and inauthentic/authentic has been erased. Fascination with the fake is as old as the imagination itself but the shift from mechanical to digital and electronic means of production and reproduction takes simulation to another level. What are the aesthetic, philosophical, social, ethical and political implications of the disappearance of what once was called real? In addition to readings and class discussions, there will be visits by an investment banker, a detective, a journalist and experts on art forgery and coun-

terfeiting. Students are required to post to a blog regularly and to participate in a weekly media lab in which they will learn how to create multimedia hypertexts and interactive websites. Instead of writing a term paper, students will be required to select an example of contemporary faking and complete a multimedia project on it. Works to be considered include: Herman Melville, *The Confidence-Man*; James Cook, *The Arts of Deception: Playing with Fraud in the Age of Barnum*; Walter Benjamin, "The Work of Art in the Age of Mechanical Reproduction"; Jacques Derrida, *Counterfeit Money*; Umberto Eco, *Travels in Hyperreality*; Andy Warhol, *The Philosophy of Andy Warhol*; Lawrence Weschler, *Mr. Wilson's Cabinet of Wonder*; and Hans Moravec, *Mind Children: The Future of Robot and Human Intelligence*. We will also study two films—Orson Welles' *F for Fake* and Christopher Nolan's *Memento*—as well as the website for the Las Vegas hotel and casino New York–New York.

This course cut across as many disciplinary boundaries as possible—class discussions probed works of philosophy, literature, art, economics and even biology. While the course as a whole has an integrity, different parts could be connected with courses in other departments. I invited a colleague from the economics department to discuss with the class how new financial instruments like derivatives related to these issues; a biology colleague helped us consider the implications of genetic engineering and cloning vis-à-vis natural organisms.

The course also bridged the divide between the academic and nonacademic worlds with two field trips. We attended an exhibition on the practice of appropriation in postmodern art and photography at the nearby Massachusetts Museum of Contemporary Art. Later in the semester we visited the restoration laboratory of the Clark Art Institute, where students learned about the scientific methods used in restoring artworks. The director of the lab, who made his reputation restoring a famous Jackson Pollock drip painting that was badly damaged in a fire, gave a fascinating talk about the legal and ethical issues involved in art restoration. What are the limits of restoration? Who determines those limits? When does the original disappear and the restoration become the work of art? When the restoration is complete, whose name goes on the work? He concluded by admitting that he took great pride in the fact that the most sophisticated computer analysis could detect no difference between his drips and Pollock's. I knew students understood what I was trying to teach them when a young woman asked, "So is the copy as good as the original and if it is, who is the artist?" I also invited a journalist, who discussed several much-publicized plagiarism cases. He explained how digital technologies and the proliferation of news outlets on cable TV and the Internet complicate questions of authorship and ownership of intellectual property. I arranged a visit by the head of the New York City Waterfront Commission, which is responsible for controlling the traffic in counterfeits and fakes. With suitcases filled with hot loot and a PowerPoint designed to shock, the police officer opened students' eyes to a vast global underworld network dealing not only in watches and fashion but more dangerously in currencies, pharmaceuticals and automobile and airplane parts.

The final assignment for the course was to create an analytic treatment of the issues we had been studying in multimedia projects that were designed for the Web. Students learned the necessary skills in a weekly media lab that was designed and taught by other students. These projects were not supposed to be merely a visual display of information, but were required to present arguments using words, images, video, sound and, above all, design. Working collaboratively in groups of three or four, students created impressive explorations of advertising and fashion, artificial intelligence, digital biology and hedge funds, as well as massive multiuser online games.

All of these projects required students to work across a range of disciplines as they never before had done. They also learned how to read difficult philosophical and literary works in ways that illuminate new media, popular culture and pressing contemporary problems without compromising academic rigor. The most impressive example of this was the project on hedge funds. One of the books we read in class was *Counterfeit Money* by the notoriously difficult French philosopher Jacques

Derrida. This work is a prolonged meditation on a one-page story with the same title by Charles Baudelaire. The students used Derrida's book and Baudelaire's story as the framework to create an interactive securities exchange that simulated online trading. They also drew on Edgar Allan Poe's short story "The Gold Bug" to show how questions of representation in literature can help us to understand the new financial instruments that now fuel the global economy. I assembled all of these projects on the interactive website we created for the course. Remaining true to the theme of the course, the interface for the site was a knockoff of the *National Enquirer*'s home page.

Of course, not all subjects lend themselves to this approach. I could not, for example, teach my seminar on Hegel, Schelling and Kierkegaard this way. Courses that use the latest media and communications technologies should supplement and not replace traditional courses. As I have stressed, it remains absolutely essential for students to learn how to read and write in traditional ways. Indeed, I am so committed to teaching young people to write clearly and effectively that I decided this would be the inheritance I would leave my children. From the summer after they finished sixth grade through the summer before they left for college, I made them write a three-page essay every week. It could be on any subject they chose, and the only requirement was that the essay had to be discursive, that is to say, they had to formulate a thesis, develop an argument, defend it and draw a conclusion. I encouraged but did not require them to write about current events or what they were reading at the time. When the essay was finished, I corrected it and went over it with them, and they rewrote it. This effort paid dividends.

But to succeed in life, young people also need to learn different ways to express themselves in other media as well. A course like Real Fakes provided the opportunity to help students think critically about the multiple media surrounding them, while at the same time learning how to use them in creative and productive ways. These Web-based projects were particularly well suited for this course. The ability to integrate written text with images, video and sound enabled students to explore the broad range of issues we examined in class in a variety of ways. Furthermore, they were able to translate their message into new media. By developing innovative designs and engaging interactive features in their projects, the students created uncertainty for the viewer or user about where to draw the line between the real and the fake in today's media-saturated network culture.

Judging by the feedback from students after the course and in the intervening years, Real Fakes was one of the most successful courses I have ever taught. The course broke down the walls that usually separate philosophy, art, economics, political science, law and biology. Significantly, students developed the ability to use new media and technologies that would be useful to them after they graduated. One of the students in the class went on to pursue a PhD in media and communications, another is working for a major advertising agency in New York City and a third manages the website for Telemundo, a Spanish-language American television network.

My experience teaching intelligent and imaginative undergraduates supports the conclusion of a recent five-year Stanford study of student writing conducted by Professor Andrea Lunsford, director of Stanford's Writing Program. In an article entitled "The New Literacy" posted on the Stanford University website, Cynthia Haven writes that contrary to conventional wisdom, Stanford researcher Andrea Lunsford finds that today's students "are writing more than any previous generation, ever, in history."

Lunsford admits that her results were unexpected, noting that her research refutes conventional wisdom and provides a response to people who ask "whether Google is making us stupid and whether Facebook is frying our brains." Lunsford began her study of 189 first-year students (about 12 percent of the entering class) in 2001. Participating students agreed to submit all the writing they did for classes, including multimedia presentations, lab reports and honors theses, along with as much of their personal writing as they were willing to share. To her surprise, Lunsford received about fifteen thousand pieces of writing, including e-mails in eleven languages. Only 62 percent of the writing was for class-work. The aim of the investigation was "to paint a picture of the writing that these young writers do" in all "its richness and complexity." Lunsford concluded that today's students are writing more than ever before, but, Haven reports, "it may not look like the writing of yesterday." Underscoring the important relationship between his work at Stanford and his writing online, one of the participants in the study commented, "The skill of being able to manage multiple, overlapping audiences is a principle of rhetoric, a skill I was able to hone and perfect not only in academic writing, but in the performance writing I did and all the rhetorical activity I was engaged in at Stanford."

Haven summarizes Lunsford's conclusions: "Today's landscape alters fundamental notions of what writing is." The most important implication of the study is "the need for higher education to adapt; for example, students could post their essays online, accommodating their preference for an audience and online discussion." But, Haven stresses, this is not enough. "Lunsford said adaptation must go even further: What does an English professor say when a student approaches her and says, 'I know you'd like me to write an essay, but I'd like to make a documentary'?" Last week a junior major in religion at Columbia came to my office and said, "I'd like to do a documentary film on Muslims in southern Russia rather than write a fifty-page paper for my senior thesis." I responded, "Then do it; but make sure your ideas are well thought out and rigorously developed and your work is carefully crafted to shed new light on the questions you probe." I was delightfully surprised when the department approved her proposal.

7

Walls to Webs

There can be no meaningful reform of higher education without redesigning departments in ways that will support more extensive collaboration among faculty members and students working in different fields. It is also necessary to make structural changes in the curriculum that will facilitate the introduction of new interdisciplinary programs focused on specific problems and themes. Departments and programs should have the openness and flexibility that allow them to adapt to the constantly evolving structure of knowledge. As I have said earlier, the explosion of information and unprecedented expansion of knowledge have resulted in ever-greater specialization that has led to increasingly autonomous departments, which are further divided into subfields within subfields. This endless fragmentation inhibits communication across departmental and disciplinary boundaries, the university dissolving into an assemblage of isolated silos. The curriculum lacks coherence, integration and overall purpose.

The challenge of effective reform is to find ways to

create a balance between in-depth study in a particular area and research on emerging problems and questions that do not readily lend themselves to a single disciplinary approach. Obviously, specialized research will always be necessary and has led to many transformative breakthroughs. Advances in medicine and the natural sciences during the past half century would have been impossible without highly specialized knowledge and sophisticated technical expertise. In recent years, however, the pendulum has swung too far in the direction of specialization, and it is now time to open avenues of investigation that cut across disciplinary lines. In many cases, the narrowing of focus is needlessly restrictive and tends to limit creativity. It often takes an outsider to see what insiders overlook. In all areas of endeavor, creativity comes about by bringing together what usually is held apart. Just as artistic innovation often occurs by mixing different genres, so intellectual innovation frequently results from crossing different disciplines. Educational reform should have as one of its primary goals the creation of conditions that make innovation more likely.

To get a sense of the problems involved with making the changes necessary to accomplish this end, consider my own field—religion. Recall the complaints of Rita, the college senior we met in the first chapter, who was looking for a graduate program in religion.

The course of study which I have proposed is inherently interdisciplinary, and I can't begin to describe how difficult it has been for me to explain this. I plan to study religion through the lens of psychology, both experimental and theoretical. I'd like to understand the impact religious specifics (texts, philosophies, rituals, etc.) through history have on the mind of the religious individual today, and how that implicates this person's behavior (from belief to going to temple/church to conversion to acts of violence). . . . I still cannot find any advisor who studies something quite like this. Despite the fact that universities may not be ready to follow this route, from talking to many future graduate students and scholars I've realized that the younger generation is craving such connections as well as applicability. Not only have I heard many people express interest in combining fields of study, but a friend and I just today discussed the implications that our psychology work (addressing evolutionary attachment and romantic relationships) could have on interpretations of religiosity.

These thoughtful comments and complaints point to difficulties in the study of religion but also reflect the obstacles to pursuing interdisciplinary study throughout colleges and universities.

When I arrived at Columbia in the fall of 2007, the department faced many of the problems Rita so articulately identifies. After conducting a survey of all graduate programs in religion in the United States, we are now developing a curriculum to overcome the fragmentation and lack of communication caused by overspecialization. The challenge is daunting: as we begin, we have ten faculty members and eight subfields—Christianity, Judaism, Islam, Buddhism, East Asian Religions, South Asian Religions, North American Religions and Philosophy of Religion. In most cases, each subfield is further divided into additional subfields. Until recently, the entire education of a graduate student from admission through comprehensive examinations to thesis was restricted to a single subfield or subfield within a subfield. In many institutions, students are able to complete a PhD in the Study of Religion by translating an esoteric text, developing a critical apparatus consisting of footnotes and cross-references, and writing an introduction. Significant linguistic requirements often take years to fulfill, leaving students little or no time to explore the breadth of disciplines and work going on in other departments that are critical for any responsible work in today's ever-more-connected world. This is typical of the way almost all religion departments across the country are organized.

The problem is not only the growing number of subfields, but also the thinking behind how they are defined. In most fields of the arts, humanities and social sciences, there are three organizational principles: tradition, history and geography. In the field of religion, major traditions are obviously important, but much of what is most interesting and significant about religion takes place outside churches, temples, synagogues and mosques and thus invariably slips through disciplinary and departmental cracks. The historical organization of knowledge has become so fundamental to higher education that it is rarely questioned, but it is laden with presuppositions that are very problematic. Needless to say, everything changes over time, but how development is interpreted varies from era to era and culture to culture.

The widely accepted division of ancient, medieval and modern is actually a theological pattern; it was first defined by Christian theologians in the so-called early modern period and continues to shape the historical imagination. But it is not clear whether this scheme should be applied to other cultural traditions. As recent historians have demonstrated, history is not a three-part story that culminates in modernity; to the contrary, there are many histories that issue in multiple modernities. The way modernity is experienced and understood in Europe and the United States differs significantly from the way it is experienced and interpreted in China, India, Iraq and Nigeria.

Traditional spatial categories are no more adequate than temporal. The commonly accepted practice of dividing and subdividing regions according to the geography of nation-states is problematic in a world becoming more and more globalized, where real space is always being reconfigured and virtual space is increasingly the sphere of intellectual and cultural exchange. Geography is one of the fundamental organizing principles for the study of religion. Subfields are defined by region—

North America, East Asia, South Asia, Japan, Africa, Europe and Russia—and then further subdivided along nationalist lines, as Buddhism is broken down into its Chinese, Japanese, Tibetan, Korean and American versions and Christianity into Eastern Orthodox, Russian Orthodox, Western, Latin American, Korean and African varieties. The situation is similar in other departments. Consider, for example, the study of literature, which is also organized by region or country in English, French, Italian, Japanese, Chinese and Russian departments. In this case, entire departments are devoted to a single language and culture. This organization is beginning to come under pressure. The University of Southern California, for example, recently announced the abolition of its German department. Rather than dividing the study of literature in this way, it would make more sense to eliminate separate departments and create a more comprehensive program in comparative literature. Such programs already exist in some schools, but they supplement rather than replace individual departments. From a student's point of view, it makes no more sense to study literature by majoring in English than it does to study religion by majoring in Christianity. Comparative study in which one literary tradition or religion is examined in relation to others is preferable to more fragmentary approaches. Research and teaching would be even further enriched by the exploration of the relationship between and among different literary and religious traditions.

In order to promote collaboration across departmental and disciplinary boundaries and to create opportunities for more experimental work, I propose extending the traditional organization of the faculty into three divisions—natural sciences, social sciences and arts and humanities—by the formal institution of a fourth division called "Emerging Zones." This new division would differ from other divisions in significant ways, promoting collaboration among faculty members and students who work in traditional departments and disciplines. These new zones of inquiry would be organized around problems and themes that lend themselves to interdisciplinary investigation. They would be designed to maximize the openness and flexibility necessary to adjust to the constantly expanding and evolving intellectual landscape. Whenever possible, these Emerging Zones of inquiry should focus on questions and problems that have practical relevance and prepare students to become responsible citizens who are capable of pursuing creative and productive careers. Bringing together people with different expertise who usually do not collaborate creates new possibilities for innovation. While novel insights and discoveries cannot, of course, be planned or programmed, they often occur through what some scientists aptly describe as "promiscuous combinations." The challenge in redesigning departments and disciplines is to establish areas of investigation that facilitate productive cross-fertilizations. This new structure would also have the advantage of providing institutional support for graduate students and young faculty members who are often discouraged by their mentors and senior colleagues from taking risks by exploring emerging areas of investigation and instead encouraged to stick to traditional subfields and methods of research.

Many colleges and universities already have what they describe as interdisciplinary programs and, paradoxically, even departments. In most cases, however, these initiatives are counterproductive because they further fragment research and the curriculum. Consider, for example, East Asian Studies, Middle Eastern Studies, American Studies, African American Studies, Gay and Lesbian Studies, Science Studies, Jewish Studies, Buddhist Studies and Christian Studies. While claiming to differ from traditional approaches, these programs are often politically motivated and quickly become as isolated, divisive and ossified as the departments they are designed to replace, rather than opening lines across disciplinary boundaries and encouraging constant change.

On a formal level, the Emerging Zones program would be university- or college-wide, and all faculty members as well as undergraduate and graduate students would be required to participate. In addition to completing a major or concentrating in a specialized field, students would have to do significant work in at least one Emerging Zone. Faculty members' contributions to these programs would play an important role in hiring, renewal and promotion decisions.

One of the obstacles to change in higher education is the fact that once departments and programs are instituted, they become permanent. I cannot recall a single time when faculty members voted to close a department. The harsh reality is that unless institutions have unlimited resources, new programs cannot be introduced without closing some departments and eliminating some programs. As I will explain in the next chapter, the problem of inflexibility is exacerbated by the policy of tenure. In order to prevent this from occurring, all programs in Emerging Zones should be approved for no longer than seven years, at the end of which they would be evaluated and discontinued, renewed or folded into other programs. The decision about the fate of a particular zone would be made by a committee that includes faculty, administrators, graduate students and undergraduates from participating departments as well as selected representatives from related departments and programs across the university.

To further enrich interdisciplinary and cross-cultural exchange, it is also important to sponsor programs like intradepartmental faculty and student seminars as well as interinstitutional conferences that create possibilities for dialogue and debate among people working in Emerging Zones and traditional departments, subfields and disciplines. Original work being done in new areas of inquiry will influence and eventually transform departments and reorient disciplines. Departments and disciplines that cannot adapt to the emerging shape of knowledge will disappear, and others will change beyond recognition.

The ideas for these changes have grown out of four decades of teaching, first at a small liberal arts college and now at a major research university. In many ways, undergraduate liberal arts institutions lend themselves to educational experimentation more readily than research universities. My experience at Williams was particularly instructive. Though my career began in the Department of Religion, for twenty-five of the thirty-six years I taught there I was not in any department and was free to collaborate with colleagues in the natural sciences, social sciences, arts and humanities. Over the years, I worked with people in philosophy, literature, history, economics, art, architecture, media, information technology and graphic design. This experience has transformed my research and publication and has led to a broad range of interdisciplinary initiatives and courses.

Though all of these collaborations have been productive, one in particular is instructive in this context. The most difficult gap to bridge, I have stressed, is the one separating the natural sciences and the humanities. The level of specialization in the sciences and the limited focus of many people working in the humanities make communication extremely difficult. And yet, it is vitally important for scientists and humanists to engage in ongoing conversation and for students to examine the difficult social, political, economic and ethical questions contemporary sciences raise. In a world threatened by nuclear weapons, bioterrorism, epidemic disease and climate change and faced with questions raised by genetic engineering, neuroscience and nanotechnology, it is essential for scientists to reflect formally and critically on the implications of their work and for students to develop the scientific literacy necessary for them to be responsible citizens. There is a growing recognition in some circles of the need to open lines of communication among scientists, humanists and artists. David Edwards, Professor of the Practice of Biomedical Engineering at Harvard, writes in his recent book, *Artscience: Creativity in the Post-Google Generation*, "Artscience [i.e., the creative synthesis of art and science] can thrive in research institutions today because science and art innovation demands the kind of culture mixing implied by crossing traditional art and science barriers. We may find the theoretical physicist turning into a material scientist, and the material scientist into a biologist. The sculptor turns into the installation artist and the installation artist goes digital."

Having worried about the problem of communication between scientists and nonscientists for many years, I proposed to teach a course that would probe questions of common concern with a colleague, Chip Lovett, who teaches in the Department of Chemistry at Williams. We borrowed the title of Austrian physicist Erwin Schrödinger's well-known book *What Is Life?* The course was not designed to explore the existential questions of late adolescents but to investigate philosophical questions raised by the latest scientific understanding of life. Chip conducts cutting-edge research on AIDS and certain forms of cancer and is the rare teacher who can explain complicated scientific theories and ideas with remarkable clarity and accuracy. His classes in our course covered the basic chemical and biological processes that make life possible, and I introduced students to different historical and contemporary philosophical interpretations of biological life. We also required students to consider some social, political, economic and ethical questions like the beginning of life, abortion, genetic engineering, cloning, psychopharmacology and euthanasia. One of the most successful parts of the course was the section we devoted to disease. Drawing on his research, Chip explained the basic biochemistry of cancer and diabetes, and I discussed recent philosophical debates about the biological and political implications of autoimmune processes. While the lectures were demanding and the readings were difficult, the response of students was overwhelmingly positive. I should also stress that this course was extremely challenging for Chip and me. It takes a serious commitment, much hard work and lots of time to reach a level of competence that allows you to teach a course like this. But after teaching the course twice, Chip and I are convinced that it was well worth the effort.

Our experience in this course can serve as a guide in designing new Emerging Zones. To glimpse how such an inquiry might be organized and how it would differ from work in traditional departments and disciplines, consider briefly two possible areas of study: the first is an extension of my work with Chip (body, health and disease), and the second grows out of a collaboration with a colleague in the Williams Department of Economics (money). In today's university, these subjects are studied in a broad range of departments and even different professional schools. There is, however, little or no effort to bring together faculty members and students in ways that integrate different perspectives and approaches. Indeed, as my former student Harvey pointed out, in medical schools, research has become so specialized that the consideration of particular organs, diseases and syndromes often preoccupies a person for his or her entire career and precludes any consideration of the body as a whole, to say nothing of broader factors related to bodily well-being. And yet, it is obvious that any adequate study of the body, health and disease requires insights drawn not only from the natural sciences but also from the social sciences (e.g., psychology, sociology, economics, political science), and contributions by schools of social work, law, business and public policy. No less important, I would insist, are the arts and humanities. Philosophy, art and literature can help people understand, treat and cope with questions related to the body, health and disease.

Consider, for example, how the problem of diabetes, which Chip and I included in our course, might be studied if it were approached in the context of an Emerging Zone. This is not an inconsequential issue, since the current epidemic of diabetes is a ticking time bomb in our health care system—scientists predict that between one half and two thirds of the children now being born in this country will become diabetic. The causes of this epidemic are not only medical but social, political, economic, environmental and psychological as well. The only way we can begin to meet the challenges this epidemic poses is by bringing together experts and professionals from all of these fields to share their knowledge and develop productive strategies. An effective program embracing the body, health and disease would encourage an integrative approach that would enrich research and teaching, while at the same time promoting more effective policies and practices within and beyond the university.

The recent financial crisis and continuing volatility of global financial markets have made it clear that we need to develop a more comprehensive and sophisticated understanding of economic processes. An Emerging Zone would be perfectly suited to this. Far too many faculty members in economics departments and business schools are enamored of physics and try to model human behavior with abstract algorithms designed to manage risk by calculating probabilities. This approach, however, leaves the human factor out of the equation. In the past couple of years, a promising new area of investigation called behavioral economics has emerged. So far, economists working on these problems have confined their research to cognitive science and evolutionary psychology. The research and teaching agenda needs to be considerably extended. Imagine how different our world might be if the people making financial decisions that impact all of our lives had studied not merely mathematical models but also history, literature, sociology, political science, anthropology and, yes, even religion. I would bet my retirement account that if Wall Streeters had read and understood Herman Melville's *The Confidence-Man*, Edgar Allan Poe's "The Gold Bug," William Gaddis's *JR*, Georg Simmel's *The Philosophy of Money* and Karl Marx's *Early Economic and Philosophical Manuscripts*, we would not find ourselves in our current economic mess.

These examples give some idea of the kind of work that could be done in new Emerging Zones. I believe large changes are needed, but realistically we have to begin modestly. The study of religion is a microcosm of broader challenges facing higher education. The problem of how to break down the walls separating eight subfields in the Department of Religion at Columbia is identical to the question of how to devise programs and structures to overcome departmental and disciplinary divisions in the broader university. During the past three years, we have redesigned the department in a way that suggests a model for a broader reform of higher education. We have begun by developing interdisciplinary programs in five zones of inquiry: Time and Modernities, Space, Transmission, Body and Media. In implementing these zones, we are bringing together people working in all the subfields of the department as well as colleagues in English, Philosophy, History, Anthropology, Latin American Studies, Asian Studies and even colleagues at other institutions like the American Museum of Natural History, the Guggenheim Museum and the University of Copenhagen Business School. The description of the Media Zone illustrates how we have defined these new areas of inquiry.

Media

(Literary, Visual, Auditory, Physical, Transportation, Information and Communication Networks)

Experience is always mediated by technologies that are constantly changing. This focus area examines how religious experience, thought, action and institutions are related to different technologies of production and reproduction. "Media" is understood in the broadest possible sense: visual (painting, sculpture, mosaics, film, photography, architecture), auditory (music, ritual, spirits), physical (bodily disciplines and practices, material factors—food, drugs, etc.), transportation (land, sea, air), information and communication (writing, mechanical, electronic, digital) and networks (social, political, economic, technological). The primary concern of inquiry in this area is to determine the ways in which religious beliefs and practices shape media and, correlatively, the impact of different media on religious ideas and life.

Graduate students still concentrate in one tradition or subfield but now are required to study with professors and graduate students working in other areas by taking courses and conducting research in one of the five zones. In a media seminar, for example, a student working on nineteenth-century American spirituality might explore the way occult religious beliefs and practices influenced Alexander Graham Bell's invention of the telephone; a student working on Byzantine theology might develop a multimedia project comparing the visual and psychological effect of church mosaics to the impact of the most recent virtual reality technology; a student studying Islam might compare the use of tape recorders by Muslims in Nigeria to the use of technology by American Christian fundamentalists; and a student working on Tibetan Buddhism might analyze research on meditation that is currently being conducted by neuroscientists. At the undergraduate level, a course like Real Fakes would work well in the Media Zone. Other examples might include a course on the relationship between twentieth-century French literature and film, the impact of iron-and-glass architecture and the rise of arcades and department stores on nineteenth-century literature and painting, and the role of ghosts and spirits in different spiritual and religious traditions. Whether at the graduate or undergraduate level, the more open, expansive and inclusive these zones are, the more effective they will be.

What faculty members teach will have to change as much as *how* they teach. Working in new ways with people not only across the university but also beyond the walls of educational institutions is required. To open new lines of communication, we offer faculty seminars in each of the zones. So far faculty members from the Department of Religion have joined with colleagues from a broad range of other departments and other cultural institutions in New York City. I am currently leading a faculty seminar as well as a graduate course in the Media Zone on a topic relevant to the argument I am developing in this book—Networks and Networking. This is a concrete example of the kind of focus area that can be explored in new interdisciplinary zones of inquiry. The following description suggests the orientation of the inquiry.

Networks and Networking

This faculty seminar will examine various kinds of networks and explore their relationship to social, political and cultural ideas and practices. Consideration will be given to the role of networks in industrial, consumer and financial capitalism through an investigation of railroads, typewriters, telephones, television, Internet, the World Wide Web and cell phones. We will also consider how networks function in living organisms (neural networks, immune systems) and natural systems (insect colonies and ecosystems). Special attention will be given to the ways in which recent theories of emergent complex adaptive systems can illuminate the distinctive structure and operational logic of networks. Do networks share a common structure? Do they function the same way in different settings? How do natural, social, economic and cultural networks interact?

I have planned the faculty seminar to bring together people in the arts, humanities, and the social and natural sciences. In addition to promoting ongoing faculty development, these seminars are intended to encourage cooperation that will result in new avenues of study for both undergraduates and graduate students. As these connections expand and relationships deepen, new courses will emerge and the curriculum will be transformed.

The response of both faculty members and graduate students to these changes has been overwhelmingly positive. The department has been reenergized, and there is growing optimism about the future of higher education in the study of religion even in these troubled times. Graduate students already are beginning to think about their research differently and are starting to consider how they can develop projects that are more inclusive and comprehensive. As these changes begin to occur, it is becoming clear that redesigning departments and creating problem-oriented programs will have another beneficial result. It will help to bridge the widening gap between teaching and research. In my own experience, teaching has always contributed to research and writing has always improved teaching. But in the culture of rarefied expertise, teaching and research tend to be set in opposition. Studying with colleagues from different fields and teaching new materials enriches research and leads to publications that will have a wider audience and be of greater relevance both within and beyond the walls of the university.

It is important to build on the considerable strengths of American higher education, while at the same time encouraging new opportunities for research and teaching. This is not change for change's sake; to the contrary, a more interconnected faculty and more flexible curriculum will promote innovation that will result in courses that are much more relevant for students in today's world. In addition to disclosing new horizons for thinking, traditional areas of inquiry will be recast in ways that show how they can actually illuminate what is going on beyond the walls of colleges and universities. Students not only need to be trained in critical thinking and conversant with the multiple cultural traditions that shape their world but also need to be adept in using the latest technology creatively and effectively. Knowledge for knowledge's sake is no longer enough; we also need to convey to students the practical import of theoretical knowledge.

Implementing these changes will make it necessary to muster resources beyond the limited means of any individual college or university. In a world of limited financial resources and increasing need and demand, former competitors have to learn how to cooperate. Just as individual departments must begin collaborating with one another, so different colleges here and abroad must learn how to cooperate. But even this will not be enough—colleges and universities must also form partnerships with nonprofit cultural institutions, local, national and international governments and even for-profit businesses. The changes that will result from these relationships hold the prospect for significant educational advantages, if they are implemented responsibly and creatively and the money is available. The blueprint for moving ahead looks something like this:

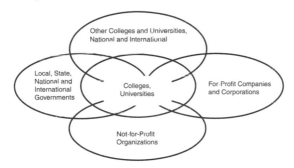

Educational Partnerships

While local, state and federal government support has been critical for both public and private higher education in America, financial pressures are straining this system to the breaking point. During a time when advanced education is more important than ever, government at every level is less able to provide much-needed financial assistance. The recent fiscal crisis in California threatens to destroy one of the world's most distinguished research university systems. The social, political and economic consequences of these developments will be felt far beyond the halls of academia as well as the state. No matter how dire the economic situation becomes, the future health and prosperity of the country will continue to depend on significant government support for research and teaching. With financial resources drying up in this country, universities and some colleges will be forced to turn to international sources for funding. In a global economy, there will be new investors in American higher education whose interests might not always coincide with the interests of those institutions. In some cases, the businessmen of education might seek to compete with colleges and universities, even when offering to cooperate. For example, a for-profit education company might partner with a university to provide online courses while at the same time developing other courses that would compete with the university's offerings. Or a pharmaceutical company might support a professor's research while independently developing competing products. In other cases, they might back research that profits their companies but does little to advance human knowledge or benefit educational institutions. These difficulties notwithstanding, it is possible to establish mutually beneficial partnerships.

Even these new sources of capital will not be sufficient to keep pace with increasing costs and declining income. Colleges and universities, therefore, are going to have to develop more creative strategies for cooperation at the local, national and international levels by forming partnerships with erstwhile competitors. These relationships should be established only if alliances allow colleges and universities to maintain or expand educational opportunities while lowering costs and increasing income. Continuing financial instability will make it impossible for institutions to do all things. In some cases, schools will be forced to concentrate their resources in limited areas and slash or even eliminate departments and divisions. While such policies are understandable, they have the undeniable effect of narrowing educational opportunities at the precise moment they should be expanding.

The only way to counter this tendency is through enhanced cooperation made possible by new media and communications technologies. In the past, cooperative arrangements were possible only for institutions sharing geographical proximity, but teleconferencing and the Internet exponentially expand the opportunities for cooperation. Some subjects can be completely outsourced; for example, let one college have a strong French department and another a strong department in German. In other cases, costs can be shared, splitting a faculty member's time between two or more institutions, by alternating physical and virtual presence. For the first half of the semester what is taught at one college can be remotely transmitted to another, and for the second half of the term this process can be reversed. This arrangement would require institutions to collaborate more closely by establishing procedures for joint appointments. Faculty members would no longer be affiliated with a single college or university and would be required to become much more mobile. But telecommunications technologies also make it possible for people to be in multiple places at the same time.

These new cooperative arrangements can be developed as effectively at the graduate as at the undergraduate level. With a dwindling number of jobs and no prospect for an increase in professional opportunities, it makes very little sense to have so many graduate programs in so many different fields and subfields. In order to consolidate resources without jeopardizing the quality of research and teaching, universities should form consortia that would allow the sharing of faculty in programs that are centered at one institution but have faculty distributed among several universities. For example, there really is no reason for all eight Ivy League universities to have doctoral programs in philosophy. Given the current state of affairs, two programs with distinctive orientations would be more than sufficient. The most effective cooperative organizational structure would be to have a core faculty constituted by select members of the home department and departments at affiliated institutions, which would be supplemented by colleagues in the undergraduate programs of all related universities. This arrangement would have the advantage of decreasing the number of graduate programs, while at the same time increasing both the number of contributing faculty members and the areas students can study. Qualified faculty members would participate in the program on a rotating basis and would always be available to serve in an advisory capacity. Courses would not be limited to offerings by resident professors but would also include lectures and seminars provided remotely. Office hours, consultations and meetings would be held using discussion and chat rooms that allow for real-time and delayed exchange and, when possible, teleconferencing. In recent years, the quality of teleconferencing has improved considerably, and it has become much more common and less expensive. When

162

the generation of technology currently in development reaches the market, there will be another significant increase in quality and accessibility.

In the absence of geographical limitations, these cooperative undergraduate and graduate programs can extend from local and regional to national and international levels. The most successful colleges and universities in the future will be *global* institutions. Many models will emerge. Schools cannot and should not try to be everywhere but will have to have significant affiliations with other colleges and universities throughout the world. This is not merely a matter of economic necessity, but also an issue of educational responsibility. For several decades, there has been much discussion about the importance of increasing the diversity of both faculties and the student bodies. Two primary justifications are offered for these policies—the first is moral, and the second is pragmatic. It is correctly argued that education at every level should be the right of all and not the privilege of a few. In the absence of increased funding for financial aid, it will be necessary to undertake new institutional initiatives to expand educational opportunities without significantly increasing costs. Beyond this ethical argument there is a more pragmatic one. If students are to become successful professionals and responsible citizens, they must develop the linguistic ability, historical background and cultural awareness that will enable them to interact with people from every kind of background and from countries all over the world.

Course offerings can be broadened and faculties and

student bodies diversified by either bringing the outside in or expanding from the inside out. The former has been the model in the past: the latter should be the new model. Colleges and universities must develop partnerships with other educational institutions throughout the world. New relationships can be established with already existing institutions. At the global as well as the national, regional and local levels, colleges and universities can undertake cooperative initiatives ranging from simple exchange programs for faculty and students to more complex arrangements that allow the joint sponsorship of curricular and administrative programs. Once again technology makes it possible to expand the number of participating faculty and to diversify both course offerings and the student body. As networking technologies continue to spread and storage capacity and speed of data transmission increase, real-time online education will become both more convenient and more popular.

Beyond partnering with existing colleges and universities throughout the world, educational institutions can serve as consultants to other governments, private organizations and investors who want to start new colleges and universities. The rising costs and growing inefficiencies of traditional educational institutions are creating opportunities for new competitors that are able to deliver high-quality education at a reasonable price. Moreover, as countries become wealthier, they want to establish their own educational institutions to meet their specific needs. In the short term, these developments offer attractive financial opportunities for American colleges and universities to provide advice and even faculty support on a fee-based work-for-hire model. The global consulting firm Mackenzie and Associates has already invested heavily in this business, but there is no reason universities can't do a much better job.

A third possibility is for colleges and universities to follow a franchise model in which they open branches in different countries. This can be done either independently or in collaboration with newly created colleges and universities, and in fact is already taking place. Qatar, for example, has created a Foundation for Education, Science and Community whose most ambitious initiative to date is the establishment of a project called Education City. The government has entered into agreements with six American universities—Cornell, Texas A&M, Virginia Commonwealth, Carnegie Mellon, Georgetown and Northwestern—to jump-start their program for higher education. The foundation website boasts: "At the heart of Education City are six universities . . . the branch campuses of prestigious international institutions that are delivering some of their most renowned programs. The availability of these world-class programs inspires young learners to strive for higher academic achievement."

In Abu Dhabi, the government has appropriated the model of the Guggenheim network to create an outstanding museum as well as a new university. Next to the site of the Guggenheim Abu Dhabi, a campus designed to accommodate the twenty thousand students who will attend New York University Abu Dhabi is rising in the desert sands. According to the mission statement, "NYU's agreement with the Emirate of Abu Dhabi to create NYU Abu Dhabi is the outcome of a shared understanding of the essential roles and challenges of higher education in the 21st century: a common belief in the value of a liberal arts education, concurrence on the benefits a research university brings to the society that sustains it, a conviction that interaction with new ideas and those who are different is valuable and necessary, and a commitment to educating students who are true citizens of the world."

These intriguing initiatives, which are bound to proliferate, create opportunities but also pose challenges. While traditional colleges and universities will continue to face major financial pressures, the global market for higher education will grow considerably. Increased cooperation among existing institutions is essential for their survival, as new players internationally become competitors. Shortsighted immigration policies that do not permit foreign students who study in this country to remain here after they complete their education will reinforce this tendency. Young people turned away from our colleges and universities will return to their own countries to conduct research and develop their own educational institutions. This is, of course, in many ways a beneficial development, since the spread of education to foreign countries contributes to the economic success that reduces poverty and promotes social justice, which in turn increases social stability. But as foreign institutions of higher learning improve, they will also become competitors that create both new challenges and new opportunities for cooperation.

Educational partnerships need not be limited to other colleges and universities but can extend to non-profits like museums, symphonies, dance troupes, think tanks and policy institutes. Since many of these organizations face the same challenges as colleges and universities, collaboration would be mutually beneficial. Cooperative programs would also provide opportunities for students to get real-world experience that will be invaluable after they graduate. A relationship between a college and a museum, for example, would provide new teaching and research opportunities for students and faculty and would benefit the museum by providing scholars and student interns who could help with programming and operations. Such collaborations can be facilitated by initiatives colleges and universities take to break down the walls between the academic and the nonacademic worlds and bridge the gulf. At Columbia, for example, we have recently opened the Institute for Religion, Culture, and Public Life (www.ircpl.org). The emphasis on public life lies at the heart of the Institute's mission. During the first two years of operation, we cosponsored programs with the Schomburg Center for Research in Black Culture, the Guggenheim Museum, the Institute of Turkish Studies and the Centre for the Study of Developing Societies (Delhi), and offered support to universities and scholars from Turkey, Indonesia, India, Israel, France, Germany, Senegal and Palestine, among others. One of the primary goals of the Institute is to create the opportunity for academics and nonacademics—writers, artists, journalists, businesspeople and government officials—to come together to discuss issues of common concern and interest. We launched the Institute with a program on the cultural, social, political, economic and religious implications of the new Guggenheim Abu Dhabi Museum. Thomas Krens, then the director of the Solomon R. Guggenheim Foundation, presented the details of the project for the first time in public. In coming years, we plan to form relationships with other cultural institutions throughout the world and sponsor joint programs using teleconferencing. As part of our outreach plan, we are developing an integrated media platform that already includes podcasts (downloadable through iTunes) as well as webcasts of Institute events and soon will be extended to include radio and television programs. I will return to this initiative in the next chapter. By creating a variety of connections between the university and the wider world, we hope to broaden the horizons of faculty and students and to educate professionals working in many areas, while at the same time informing the general public.

Finally, and most controversially, colleges and universities must establish partnerships with for-profit businesses and corporations. Let's make no mistake: higher education is a business. While we must be vigilant about the prospect of for-profit ventures exercising undue influence on institutions' academic programs, we must also be realistic about ways to respond to the financial crisis higher education is facing. A high-level university administrator recently said to me, "Going forward, those departments and divisions that can generate revenue streams will be privileged." The implications of this policy are clear: the arts, humanities and so-called soft social sciences, which produce no revenue beyond tuition, are in serious jeopardy.

There are four ways to address the problem of declining resources for many areas of inquiry: first, colleges and universities can try to raise more money from private donors as well as the state and federal government; second, they can use revenues generated by profitable departments and schools to defray the cost of unprofitable arts and sciences courses; third, they can require unprofitable departments to augment their revenue streams by increasing their teaching loads; and fourth, they can reduce the size of departments or eliminate them altogether. In the current economic climate, it is unlikely that private or public funds can be increased enough to cover growing deficits. Moreover, the reallocation of resources will not be sufficient to provide the necessary relief for distressed departments. The most likely approach in the short term is to increase teaching loads as a way of generating more tuition revenue. But this policy has inherent limitations—it is impossible to enlarge enrollments significantly without incurring additional costs not only for dormitories and classrooms but also for staff, administrators, adjuncts and graduate-student teaching assistants for whom there would have to be additional high-cost courses. It seems likely, therefore, that in the near future, some departments and programs in the arts and humanities will be eliminated and others will be reduced through merger.

There is, however, another alternative, one that is controversial among many of the very academics who most need help. Colleges and universities can establish partnerships with for-profit businesses. Most people inside and outside universities are completely unaware of the explosion in the for-profit sector of higher education. Indeed, most faculty members don't even realize the extent to which their own universities already have partnerships with businesses and corporations. In 2007, there were 2,819 such for-profit entities in the United States. This represents 41 percent of all institutions (16 percent of four-year degree-granting enterprises). All of these institutions are recognized by the Department of Education and are eligible for student loans from the federal government. The largest for-profit school is the University of Phoenix, which currently enrolls over four hundred thousand students. For-profit ventures range from traditional classrooms and combinations of real and virtual instruction to completely online programs. While the Washington Post Company's highly profitable Kaplan University and the University of Phoenix have physical campuses, most for-profit companies offer courses online, and therefore do not have expenses related to maintaining a physical plant. In addition, they do not offer the student services that traditional colleges and universities do, and they do not provide support for faculty research and development. This enables them to cycle profits back into the business and thereby expand more quickly.

When informed of the growth in for-profit higher education, most faculty members respond that such companies do not pose a threat because the education they provide is of low quality and differs significantly from what traditional colleges and universities offer. These companies are, of course, different, but they do pose a threat to traditional higher education. The rapid growth and steady improvement of online courses are making them increasingly attractive to a broad range of students. Much commercial education is now practically oriented and vocationally targeted; in most cases, the cost at for-profit schools is considerably lower than the price of education at traditional institutions. Moreover, the growing sophistication of hardware, software and multimedia programs enables for-profit companies to develop courses that can compete with some courses offered in traditional settings.

This was already evident to me ten years ago. One of the most promising projects we developed at Global Education Network was the course on American history we created for the State University of New York system. As I noted earlier, in addition to presentations by four of the system's best teachers, the course provided rich media for the students to use, which included copies of original documents, old photographs, film and video clips of major events, and an array of interactive features. When university officials reviewed the course, they agreed that it was superior to the courses most of the undergraduates took from adjuncts and professors, who did not want to teach required courses in which they had little or no interest. Using projected enrollment figures agreed upon by both SUNY and GEN, we calculated that offering the course in American history online would save the State of New York $180 million over a seven-year period. The executive committee of the board of directors of the state system also acknowledged the superior quality of GEN's course but, much to our surprise, declined to enter into an agreement because they were afraid that the New York state legislature would reduce their budget by the amount the course saved. Other institutions will not repeat this mistake in the future.

Since online courses do not require the physical presence of students in a particular place at a specific time, they allow greater flexibility, which is better suited to the needs of the changing demographics of the college population. Though the fact is rarely noted, the traditional four-year college whose students are eighteen to twenty-two years old is rapidly becoming a thing of the past. Only 16 percent of all students currently fall into this category; the majority of students are now over twenty-two. Moreover, 82 percent of college students work while going to college, and 32 percent of them work full-time. (In the early 1980s, only 12 percent of college students worked during the school year.) Flexibility is, therefore, vitally important to more and more students. Physical presence in a school with a professor in the classroom is quickly becoming a luxury that fewer and fewer students can afford, and more and more believe is unnecessary. From the fall of 2002 to the fall of 2007, online enrollment in degree-granting postsecondary institutions increased from 1,602,970 (9 percent of total enrollment) to 3,939,111 (21.9 percent). It is hard to see why this trend will not continue.

Traditional colleges and universities ignore the growth of the for-profit sector at their own peril. With costs continuing to rise and resources for financial aid decreasing, the number of young people attending four-year colleges will in all likelihood decline. Colleges and universities would therefore be well advised to form partnerships with for-profit providers that are mutually beneficial. Some individual professors and the institutions where they teach can enter into agreements with for-profit companies to provide courses that will generate income, and other schools no longer able to afford to cover some subjects can supplement their offerings by providing low-cost online courses. In this arrangement, the company gets high-quality courses, colleges and universities providing courses create another source of revenue, and schools under financial duress are able to offer students courses that would not otherwise be available. Since these courses would cost less than regular ones do, this arrangement would help reduce the expense of education.

A second way in which colleges and universities can partner with for-profit businesses is through corporate sponsorships. A successful partnership requires a formal agreement defining the benefits the corporation receives and the obligations the university incurs in exchange for financial support and, of course, vice versa. The terms of this contract must be drawn up in a way that protects the academic integrity of the university. Such corporate relationships would be a variation of the contracts between colleges and universities and the federal government that have long been an important source of income. One of the best examples of a successful corporate sponsorship program is MIT's Media Lab. According to their website,

> The Lab's primary source of funding comes from more than 60 corporations whose businesses range from electronics to entertainment, furniture to finance, and toys to telecommunications. Sponsorship provides a unique opportunity for corporations to have access to a valuable resource for conducting research that is too costly or too "far out" to be accommodated within a corporate environment. It is also an opportunity for corporations to bring their business challenges and concerns to the Lab to see the solutions our researchers present.

There are three levels of membership, ranging from $75,000 to $400,000 for a minimum of three years. The benefits to corporations include Lab visiting privileges and advisory meetings with faculty and students as well as nonexclusive, license-fee-free, royalty-free licensing rights for intellectual property.

Over the years, faculty members, students and sponsors have collaborated to introduce a broad array of products, ranging from children's toys and video games to educational programs and robotic devices for industrial use, monitoring children and the elderly and even space exploration. The Lab also has created important new technologies for the communications and computer industries. Researchers developed a new Wi-Fi (i.e., wireless technology) for Nortel as well as a new search engine for IBM designed to collect and organize information from blogs, bulletin boards, newsgroups and non-Web sources like newspapers, databases and journals. Other people at the Lab are exploring ways that computers and digital devices can be used to help people who suffer physical and mental disabilities. In 2007, the Lab held a symposium entitled "New Minds, New Bodies, New Identities." Neuroscientist Oliver Sacks, writer Michael Chorost and architect Michael Graves joined Lab faculty and students to consider how the merging of technology with bodies and minds is transforming our understanding of life and recasting the boundaries of human beings. This kind of collaboration could contribute to courses in new Emerging Zones.

Under the leadership of founding director Nicholas Negroponte, the Media Lab has undertaken an ambitious educational program. The one-laptop-per-child initiative aims to distribute low-cost computers to poor children throughout the world. A recent article in *The Economist* reports that 370,000 children in Nicaragua have received computers through this initiative. The Lab also develops and distributes educational materials that can be used on computers. One of the most successful programs for childhood education to date is the Computer Clubhouse, a worldwide network for after-school learning centers that focuses on young people in disadvantaged areas. Finally, longtime faculty member Mitch Resnick and his students are working with LEGO's electronics research and development department to develop a robotics construction set that teaches children how to use software to design different devices. Resnick reports that his lab also allows children to use a "free Scratch programming system to create stories that combine on-screen animations with WeDo constructions, allowing them to integrate virtual and physical worlds and share their stories with other children around the globe."

These partnerships between universities and companies suggest the growing range of opportunities such arrangements provide. While still in college and graduate school, students have the chance to do original research, and at the same time to work on projects that prepare them for productive careers. Many graduates begin their professional careers with the companies they worked for while in school. Much of the research at the Lab is technical, but some of it is also directed to creating content for entertainment companies and educational businesses that provide opportunities for students in the arts and humanities. It is not difficult to imagine how Resnick's work could be extended to secondary and even higher education. MIT's Media Lab offers a model for productive collaboration between higher education and business. To prepare students to take advantage of such opportunities, of course, will require training undergraduate and graduate students differently and in many cases will make it necessary to change the academic workforce.

Finally, the most extensive and profitable collaboration between universities and business is technology transfer. The Association of University Technology Managers defines technology transfer as "the practice of licensing research institution–owned intellectual property to commercial and non-profit organizations." This practice was made possible by the passage of the 1980 University and Small Business Patent Procedures Act, popularly known as the Bayh-Dole Act, which grants universities and nonprofits control over their intellectual property and inventions that result from research funded by the federal government. Under the terms of the agreement, universities can file for patent protection and are required actively to promote and commercialize inventions. Any income from inventions and intellectual property must be shared with the faculty members who created them.

Both universities and corporations were quick to recognize that this act changes the rules of the game. By the early 1990s, more than two hundred universities had established offices to market commercially viable products that faculty members created. In his book *Universities in the Marketplace: The Commercialization of Higher Education,* former Harvard president Derek Bok reports that by 2000, "many campuses had created centers to give technical assistance to small businesses or developed incubators offering seed money and advice to help entrepreneurs launch new enterprises. Several institutions formed special venture capital units to invest in companies founded by their professors." Bok's own university has been relatively slow to capitalize on this new source of income. From 2004 to 2007, Harvard made $15,881,129 on licensing and technology transfer. During the same period, Columbia University made $425,891,067. In 2007 alone Columbia's licensing income was $137,632,417, which was roughly equivalent to the entire arts and sciences budget that year. Most of this income was generated by medical devices, software and especially pharmaceuticals.

While not all universities have been as aggressive as Columbia, the overall trend is clear. Financial pressures on colleges, universities and businesses will lead to even greater growth in this sector. When these collaborations are mutually beneficial, they should be encouraged. Such agreements must, however, be carefully monitored and managed. Administrators should keep faculty members informed, and there should be an oversight committee made up of a wide range of faculty members that regularly reviews the program as well as individual agreements.

Many faculty members see these changes as a threat to the very life of higher education; I see them as opening new possibilities for research, writing and teaching that will enrich individuals and institutions in more than financial ways. No college or university can solve its problems alone. The future of higher education depends

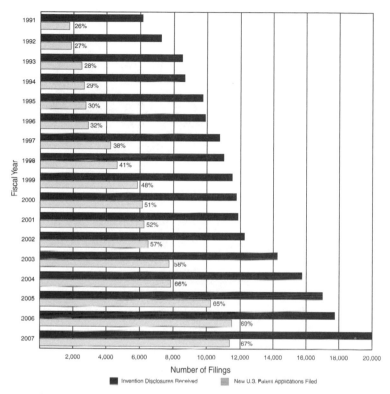

New Patent Filings and Invention Disclosures Received by
American Universities, 1991–2007

on cultivating relationships within and beyond the walls
of the academy and the boundaries of nations. In our
increasingly globalized world, colleges and universities
must work together to create a global education network that will benefit all people.

8

New Skills for a
Changing Workforce

As I have said, implementing the transformation of America's higher education system will require creating new possibilities for research and publication and recalibrating the balance between research and teaching by forming faculties that are more flexible, creative and productive. Reform is dependent on recognizing the implications of the inequitable distribution of wealth between elite colleges and universities on the one hand and, on the other, institutions with very limited resources. While a significant redistribution of financial assets is hard to imagine, a redistribution of intellectual and cultural capital is possible—and necessary—for the future health of higher education. Professors at wealthy elite schools have light teaching loads and ample time and support for research, but educators at most public and private schools labor under arduous working conditions with burdensome teaching responsibilities that leave them little time to keep up in their fields, to say nothing of conducting research and writing for publication. Though most graduate programs give students a rigorous specialized education, this training does not prepare people for a workplace in which there are few, if any, positions in the field they have studied. Ironically, many graduate programs still convey a system of values that privileges research and publication at the expense of teaching. In research universities and even many colleges, status is measured not only by how much a person publishes but by how *little* one teaches. A friend recently told me that when, a few years ago, he received a prestigious teaching award while he was working at an Ivy League university, a senior colleague advised him not to list the award on his résumé because it would demonstrate that he was not a serious enough scholar. When teaching is neither valued nor rewarded, its quality inevitably suffers.

The problem, then, is both the quality and the quantity of teaching—some people are teaching too little and others are teaching too much. Faculty members with lighter teaching loads are supposed to be conducting research and publishing original work, but only a few are truly productive; faculty members with heavy teaching loads do not have enough time to read books, let alone write them.

The emphasis on research and publication in the hiring, promotion and tenure of faculty members is a relatively recent phenomenon. As I have explained, when the job market dried up in the early 1970s and scores of people were pursuing each position, the publication of articles and books became an easy way to discriminate among the candidates. That was a mistake that led to the current imbalance between teaching and research. Publishing became desirable even if you had nothing worth saying. All this publishing led to the founding of more journals and the expansion of university presses, which, in turn, made it easier and easier to publish. Universities and many colleges began to measure their prestige by the quantity of the scholarly production of their faculties, not necessarily the quality. As publication became a symbol of achievement, ambitious colleges and universities adjusted teaching loads downward to enable faculty members to spend more time on their research and writing. The underlying assumption was that *all* faculty members not only can but actually do conduct original research and publish their results. The data do not support that assumption. In fact, very few professors remain productive throughout their careers, and many publish little or nothing after receiving tenure.

The two institutions where I have spent my professional career are typical of most top-tier schools in this respect. At Williams and Columbia, the standard full teaching load is two courses a semester or four courses per year. Each course meets once a week for two and a half hours, twice a week for seventy-five minutes or three times a week for fifty minutes. The Williams semester is twelve weeks and the Columbia semester is fourteen weeks.

This means that the total time a professor is in the classroom for the entire year is 120 hours at Williams and 140 hours at Columbia (i.e., three to three and a half forty-hour weeks per year). It is also important to note that the standard course load for students is four courses a semester and eight courses a year. Some students take additional courses, and some classes have required labs that increase class time. But many students are in the classroom between 240 and 280 hours a year (i.e., six to seven forty-hour weeks a year).

Teaching, of course, involves much more than the time one is in the classroom, but the total number of classroom hours is noteworthy. While Williams allocates faculty positions to departments based upon a formula in which each teacher is expected to instruct a total of at least 120 students a year, there is no general policy on the number of students a faculty member should teach at Columbia. The size of the classes different professors teach therefore varies widely. Since many faculty members receive course relief for chairing departments, programs and committees or use money from their research grants to pay the university to exempt them from teaching, a significant number teach fewer than four courses. In addition, faculty members at many col leges and universities are guaranteed regular leaves and sabbaticals. In most cases, these leaves do not depend on production or performance. At universities with graduate programs, graduate students teach small discussion sections in large lecture courses offered by professors, grade papers, run labs and meet with students. Advising grad students and sponsoring theses can be quite time-consuming for professors, though graduate courses typically have fewer students. Still, teaching requirements at the top schools are surprisingly low.

Now consider the problems at the other end of the

higher education spectrum. Long the envy of many states and, indeed, foreign countries, the California university system, as I have said, is collapsing under the weight of the state's fiscal crisis. Since the 1960s, higher education in California has been divided among research universities, where significant research is required and teaching loads are light; teaching universities (i.e., California state universities), where teaching loads are heavy but some publication is still required; and community colleges, where teaching loads are even heavier but there are no publication requirements. In contrast to Williams and Columbia, faculty members at California State University, Los Angeles, teach three classes each quarter and nine classes a year. While student enrollments vary from course to course and department to department, most faculty members teach roughly one hundred students a quarter, three hundred students a year. Unlike research universities, the state university provides no teaching assistants, and seniority does not reduce one's teaching load. As for the sharp dichotomy between teaching and research, a colleague at CSULA properly wrote in an e-mail,

> This distinction seems to me fallacious, since teaching and research are inextricably linked. Good teaching is founded on, among other things, the teacher's active engagement in the ongoing scholarly discussion in his or her field. And research in the humanities, because it concerns texts and issues that relate to our common

social, ethical, economic, religious and political experience, must stay connected with the transmission and exchange of ideas fostered by the classroom. I have witnessed, at our school, with a sad heart, the way that our heavy teaching load actually thwarts the putative teaching mission of the CSU system. So mind-pulping is the regimen that teachers flee from the classroom. They seek to create administrative projects and programs of doubtful intellectual worth to get "release time" from teaching. Matters are even worse in community colleges.

This is an extremely unfortunate situation because the escalating cost of higher education is driving more students to these institutions.

I gained insight into the problems of people who are teaching at schools with very limited resources from an e-mail I received from a longtime friend, Sarah, in response to my latest op-ed piece in the *Times*.

Unlike many academics, I didn't feel provoked by your *New York Times* article so much as saddened. You articulated the presence in elite research institutions of fragmentation and incoherence reeling toward educational disaster. Travel 10 miles from Morningside Heights [where Columbia is located] westward and you'll find the same fragmentation and incoherence, but at the other end of the academic spectrum:

the community college, where I teach. Here, though, these destructive elements are configured in entirely different—often diametrically opposed—ways. Compared to the Ivies, the community college is bizarro world.

I've had the privilege of struggling through both types of alienation and dehumanization, leaving me now truly untethered to anything I'd call an intellectual community. I started my academic career at Columbia, where I earned my doctorate in English, and I will end my academic career at an institution that many folks from the elite schools wouldn't even consider higher education. But it is—we are just the shameful shadow of the other. Who celebrates acceptance to community college when we have open admissions?

After all, the first community college, Joliet Junior College, in Illinois, was created in 1901 at the behest of William Rainey Harper, then president of the University of Chicago. This two-year college served the purpose of taking the pressure off of the University of Chicago to accept (less than stellar) hordes of students who wanted access to higher education.

I'll try to list what I know about my employer, colleagues, and students, much of which will be true of other community colleges.

1. By contract, faculty members teach a minimum of fifteen credits or, generally

speaking, five courses per semester for a minimum total of ten courses a year. Faculty may teach up to seven courses per semester if they wish. They may also teach in both of two intensive summer sessions. Most of my fulltime colleagues (myself included) have taught overload. There is such fear that the overload option may be taken away from them that the faculty voted down a proposal to reduce course load to four classes per semester.

2. By contract, faculty must be on campus a minimum of four days a week. We are allowed one non-teaching day. Faculty must also schedule a minimum of three office hours per week on three different days.

3. Class size is usually set at a minimum of twelve students; however, very few classes run fewer than twenty-five students and many courses run at fifty. There are often not enough chairs and class space for the number of students in certain classes. Most professors teach between 100 and 200 students per semester.

4. Faculty members do not have research assistants. Support staff is so scarce that in fifteen years I have never even asked my department secretary to Xerox anything for me.

5. My salary is the same as the very lowest starting salary for a tenure-track professor in the California state system. A full professor, I

share an office the size of a large closet with three other faculty members. This is the norm.

6. Most everyone who fulfills his/her contractual duties (which do not include publishing) will attain tenure. The faculty promotions committee has used scholarly achievement against applicants for promotion—the assumption is that engaging in scholarly work indicates a lack of dedication to college committees and student activities.

7. The rhetoric of the administration is continually about the college's mission to provide excellent teaching. And yet, many faculty members feel that if the institution were really dedicated to teaching, it would reduce the required course load, since it is next to impossible to teach five classes well per semester. Sabbaticals are not granted but rather applied for. One or two are offered to a faculty of over 400 each year.

8. The majority of all courses offered at my school are taught by adjunct professors. In the English department, they are paid $1,800 per course.

9. Our current president's goal is to double enrollment (from 20,000 to 40,000) despite the fact that there has been no doubling in facilities.

Maybe this will help give a sense of the near insanity of both ends of this current educational spectrum. It's the center that may not hold. These two ends, decapitated versions of each other, are at the moment here to stay.

After reading Sarah's e-mail, I called to ask her whether the situation she described is typical of other similar colleges, and she replied that it is. It is important to realize that state teaching universities and community colleges are as crucial to the aspirations of students attending them as research universities and elite colleges are to those privileged enough to have access to them. What is striking about the comments of both my CSULA colleague and Sarah is the pervasive tone of sadness— for themselves and their students alike. It makes absolutely no sense for this country not to commit the resources—financial and otherwise—necessary to improve the educational environment for these faculty members and students. While a significant increase in funding is essential, money alone will not solve the problem. It is also important to develop innovative programs to support overworked junior college, college and university teachers. One major question is how to bridge the gap between the rich and the poor by redistributing intellectual and cultural capital more fairly.

In order to address this growing crisis, I propose the establishment of a National Teaching Academy (NTA), which would be sponsored and funded jointly by the federal government, private donations, corporations, and leading universities and colleges throughout the country. This initiative, which should be given the highest national priority, would have enormous symbolic and practical value. While declarations of the essential importance of quality teaching are all too common, high-minded words are rarely backed by effective deeds. A National Teaching Academy, actively supported by the president of the United States and run by prominent educators, would stand as a lasting monument to the nation's commitment to the finest quality of teaching in our institutions of higher learning. To those who say we cannot afford such a bold initiative during a time of financial crisis, I say we can't afford *not* to make such a major investment in our future.

This is not the place to summarize all of the details of this proposal, but I do want to outline the general contours of the initiative. The NTA would be located in Chicago and have a loose affiliation with the University of Chicago. The central location of Chicago is clearly practical, and symbolically important in its geography, too. But there is more to that symbolism. William Rainey Harper, whom John D. Rockefeller chose to organize the University of Chicago and serve as its first president, had a vision for higher education that remains surprisingly relevant today and bears a striking similarity to some of the suggestions advanced in this book. In addition to establishing a world-class research university with an outstanding undergraduate program, Harper was, as Sarah notes, committed to expanding educational opportunities through a network of community colleges, where students spent the first two years of college. For those who could not attend classes regularly because of work or other obligations, Harper instituted the first extension service in America, fostering education at home when necessary or desirable. Were he still alive, Harper would be the ideal director of the NTA.

The primary mission of the National Teaching Academy would be to support outstanding faculty members drawn from leading colleges and universities, who would be appointed to develop high-quality seminars, classes and other programs for educational institutions that do not have the resources to underwrite proper and continuing faculty development. The activities of the Academy would be overseen by a rotating board of directors composed of administrators and faculty members from colleges and universities as well as leaders of cultural institutions throughout the country. Faculty members teaching at the Academy would be nominated by their home institutions, approved by the board of directors, and appointed by the president of the United States to be presidential fellows at the NTA for a year or two. The members of the board and the director of the Academy would also be presidential appointees.

One of the primary contributions of this program would be to elevate the status of teaching *within* universities and thereby begin to recalibrate the balance between teaching and research. Research conducted at major universities and a select number of elite colleges is, of course, critical to the expansion of knowledge and all the benefits it brings. But the unrealistic requirement that everyone engage in original research and publish his or her results creates needless pressure and leads to much work and many articles and books that are of limited use, while taking teachers out of the classroom. Many people who are unable to publish significant work or uninterested in doing so are nonetheless outstanding teachers, but they are discouraged and dispirited because they rightly believe that their contributions are neither valued nor rewarded properly. A prestigious high-profile national program would make a public statement about the importance of teaching.

But public gestures, no matter how grand, are not enough; master teachers should be paid as much as leading researchers and writers. This increase in compensation should be reallocated from the salaries of faculty members who neither produce noteworthy research nor teach effectively. The combination of increased incentives and national recognition should help to elevate the status of teaching in colleges and universities.

The students attending the NTA would come from public and private colleges and universities where faculty members carry excessive teaching loads and don't have the time or resources for continuing education, research or publication. Candidates for the Academy would be selected by their home institutions and approved by the director and board. All participants would be given at least a one-year leave from their teaching responsibilities.

Private donations and corporations would pay for the construction and maintenance of the physical plant of the Academy as well as all administrative expenses. Home institutions would contribute the salaries and cover the living expenses of the presidential fellows. The federal government would pay the salaries and provide a cost-of-living stipend for faculty members studying at the NTA.

Though the Academy's activities would be headquartered in Chicago, there would be an outreach program based at different colleges and universities scattered throughout the country. Both presidential fellows and faculty students studying at the Academy would spend one semester in Chicago, where they would take three or four courses. The courses would conform to the reorganized structure of college and university curricula. Two would focus on the field in which the faculty members teach, and two would be interdisciplinary classes that would bring together people working in different areas. For example, a professor of English might join colleagues who teach art history, political science and economics in a seminar that explores the different ways in which representation functions in literary texts, artistic works, political movements and financial markets. The purpose of all of these courses would be to give overworked faculty members the time and support to study and reflect, and thus to keep them abreast of the latest developments in fields relevant to their teaching.

These classes would be supplemented by cooperative programs with other educational and cultural institutions in the city, including the Art Institute of Chicago, Field Museum, Shedd Aquarium, Adler Planetarium, Illinois Institute of Technology, Chicago Philharmonic and Chicago History Museum. During the second semester, both presidential fellows and students would serve as visiting faculty members at other institutions, where they would offer seminars for colleagues at those schools derived from their work at the Academy. The selection of participants in these campus-based courses would be made by their home institutions and determined by both merit and interest. Faculty members would receive a one-course teaching reduction, which would be funded by government grants, to take the seminar. Particularly able faculty members who attended the Academy and proved to be unusually effective teachers would have the opportunity to become presidential fellows.

This program is obviously very ambitious—but it needs to be to meet the challenges we face. As more and more people attend the Academy and take its courses and teachers begin teaching teachers, a network will emerge that can provide continuing education and necessary support for the people charged with teaching future generations. The lack of mobility in the current job market makes it unlikely that faculty who attend the NTA will leave and makes it all the more important for colleges and universities to develop continuing education programs for their faculty.

The renewed emphasis on teaching must not, of course, detract from the continuing importance of research and publication—serious research and publication, not make-work. But here too changes must be made. Universities in the United States have long led the world in the research and development of the very technologies that are creating new opportunities to extend traditional research and publication methods and transform teaching practices. Ever since the Middle Ages, a doctoral dissertation has been meant to present original work. Graduate students in the sciences conduct research, which is often collaborative, under the direction of a "mentor" and publish their work in multiauthored articles. Humanists and most social scientists are also guided by a tenured faculty member but work in isolation and are required to produce a heavily footnoted dissertation that eventually might be published as a scholarly monograph. In practice, however, this rite of initiation produces little of lasting value.

Students working at an advanced level should not be limited to a traditional dissertation format. Monographs represent a financial failure except in the rarest of instances. Perhaps there are other formats where that won't be the case. Moreover, to compete in the workplace—academic and otherwise—students need skills above and beyond those required for producing scholarly articles and books. The best and the brightest students often feel stymied by the imposition of outdated requirements by mentors more comfortable using traditional methods and imposing their personal authority than with nourishing the creativity of young people who want to do things differently.

Working with students in media labs and on multimedia projects, I have come to appreciate alternative ways of writing and publishing. No longer constrained by words in black-and-white, ordered in straight lines and right angles, you become free to reconfigure words with any color, image or sound in designed texts that can be layered and even set in motion. Multiple narrative possibilities not afforded by the traditional book emerge. If constructed thoughtfully, texts composed in these media can reach a level of complexity that takes interpretation and critical thinking to different levels. Alternative media create great possibilities.

Mark Danielewski's remarkable seven-hundred-page book, *House of Leaves,* is a case in point. Designed around the conceit of a house that is bigger on the inside than it is on the outside, this book combines detective fiction, adventure story and psychological thriller with sophisticated philosophical analysis and literary criticism. Danielewski integrates creative and critical writing with graphic design techniques borrowed from film and video to advance the narrative of the work. The book is written in concert with a CD entitled *Haunted,* composed and performed by the author's sister, who is a rock singer and performs under the name Poe. Poe's album is "about" Danielewski's novel, which is "about" Poe's album. Adding layer upon layer, Danielewski weaves references to Edgar Allan Poe's detective fiction throughout his text. In addition to printed words and music, Danielewski designed his work to be integrated with the World Wide Web. He created a sophisticated website where he released fragments of the book and engaged in an extensive online discussion with early readers. When the book eventually was released, it appeared in several versions that were not precisely the same and used different color schemes. Ten years after its publication, www.houseofleaves.com is still a forum for lively debate about the issues this book raises. It is important to stress that this use of the Web was not simply a publicity ploy but forms an important part of the work's meaning and substance. While Danielewski is clearly the author, his multifaceted work would have been impossible without extensive collaboration. The book extends beyond its covers and keeps developing as texts on the Web proliferate. *House of Leaves* is, among other things, a haunted house, filled with ghosts, that resembles both a new kind of book and the World Wide Web. By bringing together form and content, Danielewski has created a work that mimics the structure and operation of the networks it explores and through which it is distributed and continues to be produced.

In spite of this book's originality, it would not be accepted as a thesis in any doctoral program of which I am aware. However, a flourishing industry in publishing doctoral dissertations and scholarly articles has grown up around Danielewski's work. I believe graduate programs should be willing to accept this kind of multimedia work as a doctoral dissertation in addition to theses written in the traditional way. Permitting students to work in alternative media would not only open new possibilities for creative, analytic and critical work but would also give them experience that will prepare them for careers beyond the academy in fields like entertainment, news and education.

As media expand and diversify, there is a growing need for different kinds of content that can be distributed through a variety of outlets. Major entertainment companies continue to produce low-quality programs for a mass audience. With the emergence of cable television networks, however, more serious programs with carefully targeted audiences are possible. The Discovery Channel, The Learning Channel and especially PBS already televise programs designed to educate as well as entertain. Since digital technology makes it possible to distribute content in different media, the relation between television and the Web has become virtually seamless. Television programs and websites can be coordinated in ways that complement one another. Students with advanced degrees who are technologically savvy would be prepared to work in this industry.

The so-called digital revolution has transformed the news business beyond recognition. With traditional magazines, journals and newspapers fast disappearing, it is very important for people to find new ways to collect, analyze and distribute information. Unfortunately, the increase in the volume of information has been accompanied by a decrease in the quality of the coverage. Thoughtful analysis and interpretation give way to opinion calculated to provoke. To counter this tendency, it is important for people entering news and journalism to have the requisite linguistic and historical background, cultural knowledge and critical ability as well as the experience to express their ideas effectively in media that extend beyond traditional print. If a graduate of the doctoral program in the Study of Religion at Columbia were to get a job with CNN, Fox News or *The New York Times*, I would count it a major success. But the administration of the university's graduate school regards such appointments as failures; only academic appointments count, regardless of the quality of the institution.

Another area for which redesigned doctoral programs can prepare students is radio. With the emergence of the Internet, radio has gone online. Traditional radio is losing listeners as fast as newspapers are losing readers. Recognizing the urgency of the problem, WNYC, the largest public radio station in the country, has recently diversified by purchasing three new stations and entered into an agreement with Univision, a Spanish-language television network. More important, the radio station has decided to expand its website (www.wnyc.org) and to integrate all aspects of its programming online. This new medium will offer streaming radio broadcasts from all of its four stations with additional text, images and video programming on an on-demand basis. While continuing to report the news in the traditional NPR style on the radio and online, WNYC also offers a rich array of music and cultural programs. This ambitious agenda creates the need for much more high-quality programming than the station is able to produce.

As we were developing our media program for the Institute for Religion, Culture, and Public Life, we recognized WNYC's new needs and contacted them regarding the possibility of collaborating to provide material about religion and public affairs. We are currently in the process of discussing an agreement with WNYC and have begun conversations with Public Radio International (PRI) for wider distribution of programs we develop. This collaboration would begin with thirteen one-hour programs based on events sponsored at the Institute. We are developing carefully edited versions of Institute lectures, presentations and interviews. Our first program is a series of conversations with writers on "Literature and Terror." Contributors include Salman Rushdie, Paul Auster, Jonathan Safran Foer, Uzodinma Iweala, Dalia Sofer and Philip Gourevitch. The second is a similar series of conversations with journalists, including Jon Meacham, editor of *Newsweek,* and David Shipley, Nicholas Kristof and James Traub from *The New York Times.* We are also preparing in-depth interviews for broadcast with Thomas Krens, former director of the Solomon R. Guggenheim Museum; philosopher Charles Taylor; and Pulitzer Prize–winning author Jack Miles. Our discussions have made it clear that as WNYC expands and diversifies its offerings, programs will require a rich array of written texts, images and videos to supplement audio transmissions. We are exploring ways in which we can work with graduate students and undergraduates to provide this new material. I remain optimistic that we will be able to develop innovative programs, but we face three major obstacles. The first is financial—to create programs with the production values necessary for distribution on major media outlets requires expensive equipment and people with the necessary technical expertise. We do not have adequate funds to cover these expenses and are now exploring the possibility of foundation support for our media program. The second problem is a symptom of some of the difficulties in higher education I have been discussing. While my codirector, Alfred Stepan, and I are convinced of the importance of a sophisticated multimedia program, some of our colleagues do not think this initiative is worth the money or the effort. They insist that we should be supporting more traditional programs like seminars, academic conferences and lectures, monograph publication and graduate student fellowships. These activities are, of course, important and will continue to be a part of the Institute's mission, but they are not enough. It is essential to explore new opportunities for creative expression that will result in programs that extend conversations beyond university walls. Finally, many graduate students recognize the reservations of their professors and are reluctant to devote precious time and energy to work that is not directly related to the requirements for their degree. Even when they want to develop new skills that will enable them to express their ideas in ways other than term papers and theses, they hesitate because they fear this will have a negative impact on their careers.

Here, as elsewhere, the only effective strategy is to begin modestly and grow gradually by establishing programs of unquestionable quality for the radio and the

Web. In my work with alternative media over the years, I have faced many obstacles but remain absolutely convinced that new skills will enable graduate students to contribute to the growing field of online education by working for both for-profit companies and nonprofit schools as well as cultural institutions like art museums, natural history museums, planetariums, symphonies and dance troupes. When describing some of our experiments with designing online courses at Global Education Network, I noted that such courses are a hybrid of classroom and book. One of the difficulties we faced was that while professors were very adept at traditional pedagogy they knew nothing about new media and the educational possibilities they offer. In the decade since our early efforts, hardware, software and distribution channels have improved considerably, and much more can be done now. Instead of producing courses in the traditional format and then repackaging them in alternative media, it is much more effective to design the courses using different media from the outset so that they can complement and support spoken and written course materials. To do this effectively requires research not only in traditional libraries but also in photographic and film archives, audio and video collections and the growing archive online. To produce quality educational materials, it is important to have people who have studied in graduate school involved in the production process. Crucial decisions about what students are being taught at every level should not be left in the hands of people whose interests are primarily technical and financial. More than a decade of experience leads me to believe that it is possible to establish a balance among educational, technical and financial interests that benefits both young professionals trained in doctoral programs and the companies where they work, while at the same time providing new possibilities and resources for the institutions where they studied.

In making these suggestions, I want to stress that I am not interested in technology for technology's sake; to the contrary, I am trying to find ways to use technology originally designed for other purposes to provide educational opportunities for students and generate additional professional opportunities for graduate students in a time when most of them will not be able to find academic positions. Personally, I continue to love books; indeed, I have written many and own thousands of them. Moreover, teaching small classes to gifted undergraduates and seminars with committed graduate students is one of my greatest pleasures. I realize, however, that in the future, fewer and fewer students and faculty members will have the opportunities my students and I have enjoyed. The challenge, as I see it, is to find additional ways for teachers to teach and students to study the works and subjects without which we would all be much poorer and our shared future would be darker.

To take advantage of these new opportunities it will be necessary to attract the most intelligent and inventive young people and to transform current faculties. As courses, departments, disciplines and institutions become more open and adaptable, faculty members must become more flexible so they can adjust quickly and effectively to constantly evolving networks of knowledge, incorporating useful elements from them into their teaching. The single most important factor preventing change in higher education is tenure. The only way for American higher education to remain competitive is to abolish tenure and impose mandatory retirement at the age of seventy.

During a recent conversation, the president of a small professional school said to me, "I have never been more frustrated. All but a few of my faculty members are tenured, and two thirds are well over sixty-five but give no hint of when they will retire. Everything is blocked and students are losing interest. I can't hire new faculty members who would revitalize the school. I know change is needed, but my hands are tied." There are, of course, always a few gifted teachers and scholars who remain productive into their seventies, but they are the exception. In such rare instances, it is possible to make special short-term arrangements that benefit everyone. In the case of tenure, however, there should be no exception—it must end.

Of all the suggestions advanced in this book, the abolition of tenure is the most controversial among academics. To get a sense of the impact of tenure, conduct a thought experiment. Imagine that a new company is being formed and you have been hired as the CEO. The board of directors says to you, "We want this venture to be as successful as possible. Pay employees whatever the market demands. Go out and find the very best and brightest people and hire them as quickly as possible. You have complete freedom and our full backing to assemble your team." Would you give any person, no matter how talented he or she is, a contract granting lifetime employment with no possibility of dismissal regardless of performance? If you answer yes, your company will fail and you will soon find yourself without a job. And yet, this is exactly what the policy of tenure does. After a six-year trial period, candidates are evaluated by their departments and often a panel of their peers, which recommends to the administration whether or not the person should be granted tenure. If the decision is negative, the faculty member must leave the institution within one year. If it is positive, the person is granted tenure and usually promoted to the rank of associate professor. Four to six years later there is a review for promotion to full professor. Once tenure is granted, there is no possibility of dismissal except in cases of egregious ethical transgression or criminal activity.

The traditional defense of tenure is academic freedom. In the absence of tenure, the argument goes, professors would not be free to express controversial ideas, new ideas that question conventional wisdom, without fear of dismissal. But on the basis of my experience, this argument is completely without merit—in forty years of teaching, I cannot think of a single person who was more willing to express his or her views after tenure than before. Less noble motives actually lie behind the impassioned defense of tenure. Further, tenure more often reinforces the status quo than encourages new ideas.

The practice of tenure was introduced to American higher education in 1915 by the American Association of University Professors (AAUP) and was reaffirmed in the "1940 Statement of Academic Freedom and Tenure," which remains the accepted norm governing colleges and universities. If one reads this document carefully, it becomes clear that the justification for tenure is not as pure as its defenders claim.

> Tenure is a means to certain ends; specifically: (1) freedom of teaching and research and of extramural activities, and (2) a sufficient degree of economic security to make the profession attractive to men and women of ability. Freedom and economic security, hence, tenure, are indispensable to the success of an institution in fulfilling its obligations to its students and to society.

The two justifications for tenure, academic freedom and economic security, are not even weighted equally. Elsewhere in the 1940 document, the AAUP insists that *all* faculty members, tenured and untenured alike, should be granted academic freedom, making clear that tenure is hardly a prerequisite for academic freedom. Proponents of tenure never explain why the freedom of speech protected by the First Amendment, which is good enough for everybody else, is not adequate for them.

Tenure is not primarily about academic freedom; it's about job security and economic well-being. Why should tenured professors enjoy lifetime employment and the economic security it brings no matter how well or poorly they perform or how productive they are? It is long past time for faculty members to rise above narrow self-interest, give up the doctrine of academic exceptionalism and agree to the same terms of employment as everyone else in the workforce. Tenure has not always existed and is not the policy everywhere. England, for example, abolished tenure for all new appointments in 1988, and their system of higher education has hardly collapsed.

Tenure imposes costs both economic and educational. Let's return to the analogy between financial capital on the one hand and, on the other, intellectual and cultural capital. It now becomes clear that tenure is a li quidity issue. Financially, declining assets and income combined with rising debt and expenses are making it increasingly difficult for colleges and universities to meet their ongoing financial obligations. Tenure is expensive. Take as the point of departure the average salary and benefits for a newly tenured faculty member at a private or public school, and make two assumptions: one, the person will be an associate professor for five years and a full professor for thirty years; two, salaries will increase at an annual rate of 3.5 percent. The total financial commitment for tenuring a professor at a private school will therefore be $12,198,578, and at a public school, $9,992,888. The endowment currently required to fund these positions is $3,959,743 and $3,252,426, respectively. Assuming a growth rate of 6 percent, the endowment necessary to support the tenured professor by the time of his or her retirement would be $28,721,197 (private) and $23,583,423 (public). These calculations include only salary and benefits and not related expenses like office space, secretarial support and research funds, which can cost additional tens or even hundreds of thousands of dollars each year. In fact, this represents the minimum expense incurred, since many tenured faculty members are paid much more than I assume here.

Two factors must be clearly distinguished in calculating the economic cost of tenure. One is the actual annual financial outlay and the endowment required to support it, and the other is the loss of liquidity that a tenure commitment imposes. With endowments plunging, and excessive debt and fixed costs rising, tenure creates a loss of financial flexibility just when it is most needed. The tenure system is financially punishing.

Even if tenure can be funded, it should be abolished. Illiquidity is as much a problem for intellectual and cultural capital as it is for financial capital. When intellectual assets are frozen, colleges and universities suffer. Once tenure is granted, there are no incentives to encourage faculty members to continue to develop and remain productive; nor is there any leverage to force them to do what they would prefer to avoid, even when it is good for the institution. Any unbiased observer would have to admit that it is simply impossible to predict whether an area of expertise that seems important today will be relevant in five years, to say nothing of thirty-five years. Nor is it possible to anticipate how promising scholars and teachers will perform in the future. In education as in finance, there is no such thing as a sure bet. It makes absolutely no sense for a college or university to make lifetime commitments to faculty members whose performance can be neither predicted nor modified. To be able to adapt to a rapidly changing world, it is essential for higher educational institutions to maintain flexible workforces. Tenure does not further that goal.

A mandatory retirement age must also be addressed. With increasing longevity and growing personal financial insecurity, many faculty members are deferring retirement longer and longer. Indeed, it is not uncommon for teachers to stay at work well into their seventies. This growing tendency leads to both financial and intellectual difficulties. In almost all cases, the more senior the person, the higher the salary. The deferral of retirement, therefore, creates additional pressure on limited budgets. There are intellectual problems, too. To be candid, on campuses, the best work of people in their late sixties and seventies is behind them. With rare exceptions, aging faculty members either rewrite previous books or produce nothing at all, and in the classroom they recycle notes they have used for many years. Faculty members who refuse to retire almost always hold positions that would be better filled by young people. When I discuss these difficult problems with graduate students, I am struck by how many insist that they would gladly trade the prospect of guaranteed lifetime employment with no mandatory retirement for the opportunity to compete for jobs that the very tenured professors training them are blocking for the foreseeable future. Though their perspective might change if they get a job, most of them will never hold an academic position. I believe we should take their opinions seriously.

A viable system for appointment, review, promotion and dismissal must fit the new organizational structure of colleges and universities and must be designed to adapt to their ongoing evolution. Just as fixed departments and rigid disciplines should be loosened up to make room for new programs in emerging fields that are approved for no longer than seven years, so permanent faculty contracts should be discontinued and replaced with seven-year contracts whose renewal or termination depends on performance-based evaluation. These reviews must be serious, not perfunctory. While the criteria used in making assessments will, of course, vary from institution to institution and department to department, there should be a general commitment to supporting faculty whose work cuts across traditional departmental and disciplinary boundaries (one or more of the Emerging Zones) as well as outstanding work in a particular field (established disciplines).

Shifting criteria for evaluation will lead to changes in the people making personnel decisions. The current review process resembles a rite of initiation into a private club that is far from an open and fair evaluation process. The practice of peer review, which, like so much else, dates back to Kant, establishes a closed system that is self-reinforcing and self-perpetuating. Experts pass judgment on colleagues in the same subfield whose acknowledgment and deference establish the experts' own authority. While intended to protect objectivity and ensure the quality of the work evaluated, the secrecy of the peer review system creates the possibility of arbitrary and self-interested judgments. Moreover, this closed system discourages people from taking risks by doing innovative work.

In her insightful study entitled *How Professors Think: Inside the Curious World of Academic Judgment* (2009), Michèle Lamont comments on the contrast between the ideals and the reality of the peer review process. Reviewers, she explains, "bring into the mix diversity considerations and more evanescent criteria—elegance, for example. These rules include respecting the sovereignty of other disciplines and deferring to the expertise of colleagues." This deference to expertise has a chilling effect on anyone whose work is critical of established authorities or transgresses traditional disciplinary boundaries. "Going against the tide in any endeavor," Lamont continues, "is often difficult; it may be even more so in scholarly research, because independence of thinking is not easily maintained in systems where mentorship and sponsored mobility loom large. Innovators are often penalized if they go too far in breaking boundaries, even if by so doing they redefine conventions and pave the way for future changes."

If these problems are to be overcome, it is necessary to open the review process by expanding it beyond experts in the field or subfield to include people working in relevant programs in the Emerging Zones division. In practice, this would mean having a review committee that includes members of the person's department and experts from other institutions as well as colleagues working in the Emerging Zones to which the candidate contributes. Current and projected research and teaching in both the department and the zone should be judged equally. If the candidate's work is deemed acceptable and if it is reasonable to expect that he or she will remain productive, a contract should be renewed for seven years. If the work is unsatisfactory, the person's contract should be terminated. By opening the review process and limiting the duration of contracts, institutions can maintain the flexibility necessary to protect financial, intellectual and cultural liquidity.

In spite of the magnitude of the crisis higher education is facing and the urgent need for change, I do not think tenure should be revoked for those to whom it has already been granted; I don't believe it is fair to change the rules in the middle of the game. Rather, colleges and universities need to find ways to encourage faculty members who are no longer productive to retire. Unfortunately, financial constraints make it impossible to use the preferred method in the business world; most schools simply cannot afford to offer faculty members attractive buyout options.

An alternative strategy would be a variation on the

merit pay system that most colleges and universities claim to follow. In its current form, merit pay represents increased compensation for above-average performance, but the pay differential usually is so small that it makes little difference. There is no reason this system cannot be made a two-way street by creating disincentives for unproductive faculty members to continue teaching. If faculty members can be rewarded for outstanding performance with increasing salaries, people who are not performing well can be penalized by decreasing their salaries. During the transitional period while tenure is being phased out, it would be possible to begin by reducing a faculty member's salary by 15 percent and imposing an additional 10 percent reduction every year he or she refuses to retire. Since retirement income is often calculated on the basis of a person's average salary for the past five years he or she has worked, it wouldn't take long for this policy to have an impact. The money saved could be used to reward people who are productive and to hire new faculty capable of doing innovative work.

Needless to say, these measures will be vehemently opposed by tenured faculty members and most likely could not be implemented by any college or university acting alone. While some informed administrators and trustees privately acknowledge that the tenure system is undesirable and unsustainable, they will not admit so publicly to avoid confrontation. The only way tenure will be abolished is if a group of leading public and private colleges and universities act together to change the system. The reality is that faculty members are in no better position to resist such an initiative than the autoworkers' union is to oppose changes in Detroit.

From a broader perspective, the alternative plan I am proposing has multiple advantages. By holding all faculty members to the same high standard, regular performance reviews would actually be fairer and would introduce more accountability, which would result in greater creativity and productivity. This system would also open the faculty ranks to young people and other groups who have been excluded for more than three decades by entrenched tenured faculty members. Greater financial and curricular flexibility would enable colleges and universities to maintain rich and diverse programs that could effectively adapt to changing circumstances and prepare students for a broad range of careers.

9

Class of 2020

To repeat what I said earlier, American higher education is at a tipping point. Events across the globe are conspiring to create instabilities that call into question centuries-old traditions and threaten the very survival of some of our most venerable educational institutions. Until very recently a world without newspapers in which well-established companies went bankrupt and major financial firms disappeared in a few days was inconceivable. This turbulence is creating growing problems for colleges and universities. All institutions of higher learning are facing major cutbacks; many are stretched to the breaking point and some are already failing. These problems are not limited to marginal institutions but extend to some of our nation's leading public and private colleges and universities. The venerable California university system is being dismantled, and Harvard's misguided investments and imprudent decisions raise questions about its financial solvency.

While many American colleges and universities are contracting, other countries, especially in Asia, are investing heavily to expand higher education. In a recent article entitled "America Falling: Longtime Dominance in Education Erodes," published in *The Chronicle of Higher Education*, Karin Fischer writes:

> Whether the current system, if unchanged, can weather recessionary storms and increased competition from overseas is an open question. Unlike their counterparts in Asia, Americans have simply not felt the urgency to reinvigorate and reinvest in higher education as a means to better position the country in a competitive and shifting global economy, says Charles M. Vest, president of the National Academy of Engineering and a former president of the Massachusetts Institute of Technology.

In such an environment, the unthinkable becomes thinkable. What if Harvard were to fail? When the next financial crisis hits—and there will be another one bigger than the last—Harvard might not have sufficient liquid assets to service its staggering debt and might be unable to make enough cutbacks to remain solvent. In this situation there are four possibilities: Harvard could declare insolvency and close its doors; the university could seek a government bailout; creditors could take over the university and sell its assets—financial and otherwise—to recover some money for investors; or creditors could sell Harvard's debt to China or another country, which would then assume control of Harvard. Impossible? So was the bankruptcy of General Motors.

The problems facing colleges and universities are not only financial. The two-hundred-year-old industrial model that remains the foundation of their organization and operation is inadequate in today's fast-changing networked world. The inability to adapt quickly and effectively is making it increasingly difficult for colleges and universities to provide the kind of education people need. The outdated ideal of faculty, departmental, disciplinary and institutional autonomy must give way to cooperative associations that extend from the local to the global. The people and institutions willing and able to adapt to these changing circumstances will thrive, and those that resist change will quickly become obsolete.

Many of the changes we have been considering are likely to accelerate in the near future and to lead to a major transformation of higher education in the next decade. Traditional instruction in colleges and universities will continue but will become less affordable and therefore less accessible. Older, more diverse and more mobile students will demand education more directly related to their personal and professional needs and will require new means of delivery. Fewer students will be eighteen to twenty-two years old and more people will take courses intermittently throughout their lives. Higher education, like everything else, will become increasingly global. Colleges and universities will not remain autonomous but will be networked with other institutions around the world to create a global education network that holds the promise of improving and enriching human life.

It is, of course, important to recall Yogi Berra's warning, "It's always risky to make predictions—especially about the future." But projections are unavoidable; human life is unimaginable without a vision of the alternative futures toward which we might move. So let me conclude by offering a sketch of what life might look like for a member of the class of 2020.

Luke is now in the sixth grade and, like most eleven-year-olds, lives in the virtual as much as the real world. Unlike in previous generations, his networks extend beyond family, school and neighborhood to other countries throughout the world. His parents worry that he spends too much time online, but Luke says that he learns more about China, Ghana, Poland, Argentina and Iceland from e-mail and the Internet than he does from his teachers in school. He constantly pesters his parents to let him join social networks like Facebook, MySpace and Ning, which is for the moment the newest new thing in social networking. His parents resist, saying he is too young, but it's not clear how long they will stand up to the pressure.

Looking ahead three years, we find Luke and his family living in a small Midwestern town still paying for the 2008 financial meltdown with higher property taxes and lower school budgets. When he begins high school, Luke discovers that advanced placement courses have been eliminated. College-bound students and their parents raise an uproar, and the school board responds by cutting a deal with a for-profit company that provides high-quality online courses in the humanities and sciences for a bulk rate of only $100 a course. This arrangement is more attractive than traditional classes because most colleges and universities across the country give credit for courses taken from this company.

Having tracked developments in the Middle East on the Internet since he was ten, Luke decides to take an online course on Islamic religion. Coming from the Midwest and never having been outside the United States, he knows nothing about Islam but realizes it is important for his future. Luke is immediately captivated and finds the teacher one of the best he has ever had. As his interest grows, he spends more time online learning as much as he can about Islamic culture. His journey starts in the Middle East and takes him to Central Asia, the Balkans, Indonesia, Africa and even cities in his own country that have significant Muslim populations. At every stop along the way, Luke meets new people and makes new friends, his social network growing faster than ever. He is surprised not only by their differences but also by how much they share. His new friends like many of the same films and much of the same music, and have many of the same fears and hopes that he does.

When it comes time for the traditional family college tour the summer after his junior year, Luke demurs. Having graduated from top colleges, his parents are disconcerted and insist that in today's highly competitive world, education is more important than ever. Luke says he knows the value of education but is not convinced that a traditional four-year college is best for him. He tells his parents that he wants to start his education at

New York University Abu Dhabi and end it online. Luke explains that, while surfing the Web for his Islamic religion class, he stumbled on the NYU Abu Dhabi website and knew immediately that this was the school for him. It is now fully operational and has been accepting students for five years. What makes NYU Abu Dhabi even more appealing is that it is located on Saadiyat Island right next to Frank Gehry's spectacular new Guggenheim Abu Dhabi. NYU and the Guggenheim have a cooperative arrangement that enables museum employees to take courses at NYU and students to participate in an extensive internship program at the museum, which introduces them to every department. Interns not only work with artists, architects, curators and designers but also with people in administration, development, education and public relations. Luke is particularly interested in the Guggenheim's collaboration with Apple, Sony and Google in the new art and technology program. One of the strengths of NYU Abu Dhabi is its interdisciplinary program in new media. By selecting courses that will help with his work at the Guggenheim, Luke hopes to avoid the problem of paying $329,000 (which will be the cost of college for the class of 2020) for an education that leaves him unemployed.

Luke insists that he doesn't need four years at NYU Abu Dhabi—he figures two will be enough. He has heard that the Guggenheim is starting a new museum in Kazakhstan that will focus on Islamic art. An American museum with a Jewish heritage working with the government of a country with a majority Muslim population that was a part of the former Soviet Union to create a Guggenheim Kazakhstan devoted to Islamic art—who would not want to get in on the ground floor of that operation? If Luke discovers that he needs more education, he will take online courses from the company that introduced him to this exciting new world. He continues to watch their course offerings and sees they are expanding and getting better all the time. Luke expects to be taking courses his whole life, and there is no way to know now what he will need to study in the future. Furthermore, he never expects to settle down and live in one place for more than a couple of years and so needs educational opportunities as flexible as he is mobile.

This scenario is not fanciful; indeed, much of it is already available to anyone who is aware of how quickly higher education is going global. And yet most people working in colleges and universities refuse to accept the way the world around them is changing. The few who do realize that schools no longer can operate as they have in the past often become discouraged by the resistance of entrenched interests and declare the situation hopeless. But complacency and hopelessness are luxuries we cannot afford. Though the times undeniably are tough, we have the intellectual, cultural and financial resources to meet the formidable challenges that lie ahead. It is clear what's wrong with higher education. The only question is whether we have the vision and will to fix it before it is too late.

Acknowledgments

This book has grown out of nearly four decades of teaching, writing, thinking and experimenting. Along the way I have become indebted to many colleagues, students and friends. I would like to offer a special word of thanks to my former faculty, administration and staff colleagues at Williams College and especially the Office for Information Technology, which actively supported all of my ideas no matter how crazy they were. Though many students have helped me over the years, José Márquez and John Kim first introduced me to possibilities I had never imagined. At Columbia University, my colleagues in the Department of Religion and at the Institute for Religion, Culture, and Public Life have enthusiastically joined in a sustained effort to introduce institutional and curricular changes we hope will enrich higher education. None of this would be possible without the support of Nicholas Dirks, vice president for arts and sciences, and Henry Pinkham, dean of the graduate school.

John W. Chandler became the president of Williams College the year I arrived as a young assistant professor.

Over the years we have become close friends, and I still turn to him for his sage counsel.

My work with Esa Saarinen, who taught philosophy at the University of Helsinki and is currently a professor at Helsinki University of Technology, was formative, and we have sustained our conversation for two decades. In 1998, I cofounded Global Education Network, and many of the ideas developed in this book grew out of that endeavor. I am particularly indebted to my colleagues at GEN, Herbert A. Allen Jr., Herbert A. Allen III, Steven Greenberg, Alexander Parker, Jon Newcomb and Kim Wieland for their interest and support.

As always, the tireless efforts of Margaret Weyers make it possible for me to do all I do.

I am especially privileged to work with Laurence J. Kirschbaum and Meg Thompson, who know their way around the New York literary scene like few others.

If David Shipley had not published my op-ed in *The New York Times,* this book never would have been written. David was in a class of mine on religion at Williams College many years ago, and I have followed his career with interest. His distinguished work offers ample evidence of the lasting value of liberal learning.

During a recent conversation, a friend who is an experienced writer and accomplished journalist said to me, "Editors no longer edit; they spend all of their time going to lunches and dinners with the hope of finding authors and manuscripts." I am fortunate enough to have an editor who not only edits but *really* edits. Jonathan Segal originally suggested that I write this book and has consistently demonstrated an extraordinary commitment to it. He has pushed and pushed me to express my ideas clearly and accessibly, and if I have succeeded, it is in no small measure because of Jon. Jon's unusually able colleague Joey McGarvey has also made many valuable suggestions and contributions.

There is no one with whom I have had a longer and more meaningful friendship and a more sustained intellectual dialogue than Jack Miles. We began talking over forty years ago, and hardly a day goes by that we don't communicate. Jack reads and responds to everything I write and his comments always improve my work. Like all true friends, Jack is willing to tell me what I don't want to hear.

Finally, I want to thank my family: my brother, Beryl, with whom I learned the virtues of teaching from our parents, who were lifelong teachers; my wife, Dinny, who is always the one who first reads what I write and who has taught me most of what I know about technology and much else; our daughter, Kirsten, our son, Aaron, and his wife, Frida, who began as my students and have become my teachers.

I have dedicated this book to our grandchildren, Selma Linnea Taylor and Elsa Ingrid Taylor. Their future as well as the future of children throughout the world in no small measure depends on our ability and willingness to fix higher education.

—M.C.T., November 2009

Notes

2. Beginning of the End

30 "There has never been a year": Mark Kurlansky, *1968: The Year That Rocked the World* (New York: Ballantine Books, 2004), xvi–xvii.

35 "There is one thing": Allan Bloom, *The Closing of the American Mind* (New York: Simon & Schuster, 1987), 25.

36 "The students' wandering and wayward energies finally found": Ibid., 50–51.

36 "an academic version of Oliver North": http://www.answers .com/topic/allan-bloom.

41 Nationally, from 1975 to 1987: Frank Donoghue, *The Last Professors: The Corporate University and the Fate of the Humanities* (New York: Fordham University Press, 2008), 32.

3. Back to the Future

51 "Whoever it was that first": Immanuel Kant, *The Conflict of the Faculties*, trans. Mary Gregor (Lincoln: University of Nebraska Press, 1979), 23.

53 "While only the scholar": Ibid., 27.

61 "In my master's program": Jennifer Williams, "Hard Work, No Pay," *The New York Times*, October 4, 2009.

64 "unforced and non-purposeful": Quoted in Charles E. McClelland, *State, Society, and University in Germany, 1700–1914* (Cambridge: Cambridge University Press, 1990), 118–19.

65   "called on Harvard to reform": Quoted in Frederick Rudolph, *The American College and University: A History* (New York: Knopf, 1962), 236.

65   "We need to produce": Quoted ibid., 65.

66   "We have cheapened education": Quoted ibid., 219.

66   "engage in mercantile": Quoted ibid., 135.

66   "purposefully obliterating": Quoted ibid., 331.

4. Emerging Network Culture

72   "This generation swallowed computers": Quoted in Theodore Roszak, *The Cult of Information: The Folklore of Computers and the True Art of Thinking* (New York: Pantheon, 1986), 150.

5. Education Bubble

91   "These findings suggest": David Swensen, *Pioneering Portfolio Management: An Unconventional Approach to Institutional Investment* (New York: Free Press, 2000; revised 2009), 58.

93   "On December 16, 2008": http://www.insidehighered.com/views/2009/04/09/wolfston. © 2009 James H. Wolfston Jr. All rights reserved.

95   "There are going to be a hell of a lot": Nina Munk, "Rich Harvard, Poor Harvard," *Vanity Fair,* August 2009, 108, 111–12.

95   "The first Faculty meeting": Bonnie Kavoussi and Lauren Kiel, "Faculty Meeting Lacks Usual Cookies," *The Harvard Crimson,* October 7, 2009.

97   "To give themselves financial breathing room": Andrew Bary, "The Big Squeeze," *Barron's,* June 29, 2009.

98   an astonishing two thirds: Goldie Blumenstyk, "Debt Bomb Is Ticking Loudly on Campuses," *The Chronicle of Higher Education,* April 10, 2009.

99   stripped of its triple-A rating: Craig Karmin, "Big Moan on Campus: Bond Downgrades," *The Wall Street Journal,* May 29, 2009.

101   According to a 2009 Congressional report: *Fortune,* April 27, 2009.

102   "It would be reasonable": http://www.finaid.org/savings/tuition-inflation.phtml.

105 **"How much does a college education"**: David Leonhardt, "The College Calculation," *The New York Times*, September 24, 2009.

6. Networking Knowledge

114 **"Everlastingly chained"**: Friedrich Schiller, *On the Aesthetic Education of Man in a Series of Letters*, trans. E. M. Wilkinson and L. A. Willoughby (New York: Oxford University Press, 1967), 35.

137 **"are writing more than any previous generation"**: Cynthia Haven, "The New Literacy: Stanford Study Finds Richness and Complexity in Students' Writing," *Stanford Report*, October 12, 2009.

7. Walls to Webs

149 **"Artscience can thrive"**: David Edwards, *Artscience: Creativity in the Post-Google Generation* (Cambridge, Mass.: Harvard University Press, 2008), 69.

172 **Only 16 percent of all students**: Donoghue, *The Last Professors*, 89–90.

173 **From the fall of 2002**: "Insider Insights on the Growth Economy," *Next UP!* vol. 4, issue 18, www.nextupresearch.com, May 17, 2009.

176 **"free Scratch programming system"**: http://www.media.mit.edu.

177 **"many campuses had created centers"**: Derek Bok, *Universities in the Marketplace: The Commercialization of Higher Education* (Princeton: Princeton University Press, 2003), 12.

178 **From 2004 to 2007, Harvard made**: *AUTM U.S. Licensing Activity Survey, FY2007: A Survey Summary of Technology Licensing (and Related) Activity for U.S. Academic and Non-profit Institutions and Technology Investment Firms*, ed. Dana Bostrom, Robert Tieckelmann and Richard Kordal, Association of University Technology Managers website, www.autm.net.

8. New Skills for a Changing Workforce

207 **Take as the point of departure:** These are my own calculations.
211 **"bring into the mix":** Michèle Lamont, *How Professors Think: Inside the Curious World of Academic Judgment* (Cambridge, Mass.: Harvard University Press, 2009), 6, 10.

9. Class of 2020

216 **"Whether the current system":** Karin Fischer, "America Falling: Longtime Dominance in Education Erodes," *The Chronicle of Higher Education,* October 5, 2009.

Index

Page numbers in *italics* refer to tables and graphs.

231

Index

Index

Index

Index

PERMISSIONS ACKNOWLEDGMENTS

Grateful acknowledgment is made to the following for permission to reprint previously published material:

Barron's: Excerpt from "The Big Squeeze" by Andrew Bary (*Barron's,* June 29, 2009). Reprinted by permission of *Barron's.*

The Chronicle of Higher Education: Excerpt from "America Falling: Longtime Dominance in Education Erodes" by Karin Fischer (*The Chronicle of Higher Education,* October 5, 2009), copyright © 2009 by *The Chronicle of Higher Education.* Reprinted by permission of *The Chronicle of Higher Education.*

The Harvard Crimson: Excerpt from "Faculty Meeting Lacks Usual Cookies" by Bonnie Kavoussi and Lauren Kiel (*The Harvard Crimson,* October 7, 2009). Reprinted by permission of *The Harvard Crimson.*

Nina Munk: Excerpt from "Rich Harvard, Poor Harvard" by Nina Munk (*Vanity Fair,* August 2009). Reprinted by permission of Nina Munk.

The New York Times: Excerpt from "Cracks in the Future" by Bob Herbert (*The New York Times,* Editorial Section, October 3, 2009), copyright © 2009 by *The New York Times;* excerpt from "The Way We Live Now: The College Calculation" by David Leonhardt (*The New York Times,* Magazine Section, September 27, 2009), copyright © 2009 by *The New York Times;* and excerpt from "Hard Work, No Play" by Jennifer Williams (*The New York Times,* Editorial Section, October 4, 2009), copyright © 2009 by *The New York Times.* All rights reserved. Reprinted by permission of PARS International Corp., on behalf of *The New York Times* and protected by the copyright laws of the United States. The printing, copying, redistribution or retransmission of the material without express written permission is prohibited.

A NOTE ABOUT THE AUTHOR

Mark C. Taylor is Professor of Religion, chair of the Department of Religion and codirector of the Institute for Religion, Culture, and Public Life at Columbia University; Professor of Philosophy of Religion at Union Theological Seminary; and Professor Emeritus of Humanities at Williams College. He received his BA from Wesleyan University and a PhD in Religion from Harvard University, and was the first foreigner to be awarded a Doktorgrad in Philosophy from the University of Copenhagen. His many awards include a Guggenheim Fellowship, the University of Helsinki's Rector's Medal and Wesleyan University's Distinguished Alumni Award. In 1995, the Carnegie Foundation named him National Professor of the Year for his use of technology to advance higher education. His most recent books include *Field Notes from Elsewhere: Reflections on Dying and Living, After God, Confidence Games: Money and Markets in a World Without Redemption* and *Mystic Bones*. He lives in Williamstown, Massachusetts, and New York City.

A NOTE ON THE TYPE

This book was set in Minion, a typeface produced by the Adobe Corporation specifically for the Macintosh personal computer and released in 1990. Designed by Robert Slimbach, Minion combines the classic characteristics of old style faces with the full complement of weights required for modern typesetting.

Composed by North Market Street Graphics,
Lancaster, Pennsylvania
Printed and bound by RR Donnelley,
Harrisonburg, Virginia
Designed by Virginia Tan